The Restaurants in Barbados

Published by Wordsmith International

Photography - Mike Toy

Design - Eightzeronine Design Associates Inc.

Distributed by Miller Publishing Company
Edgehill, St.Thomas, Barbados, West Indies.
Tel: (246) 421 6700 Fax:(246) 421 6707
E-mail: miller@caribsurf.com

Printed in Singapore

ISBN 976 - 8079 - 77 - 0

Contents

Barbados offers an eclectic selection of superb and truly international standard restaurants that is quite disproportionate to its physical status as a remote Caribbean island of a mere 166 square miles. Measuring just 21 miles by 14 miles at its widest points, and with a population of around 265,000 people, Barbados is comparative in size to what would be considered a small town in Europe or North America. Yet, quite contrary to these modest proportions, this special island is home to a wide and varied range of excellent restaurants, offering a host of tasty, local speciality dishes and the full gamut of international cuisines.

While acknowledging the outstanding quality of everyday Barbadian food and recognising the culinary skills of thousands of Bajan cooks, we have opted to focus the spotlight on a selection of the more accomplished restaurants that have consistently distinguished themselves by virtue of their good food, good ambience and good service, all of which are on a par with generally accepted international standards. With so many restaurants open on the island today it is impossible to include them all in a book of this nature, so we have unfortunately been obliged to omit some establishments. Please rest assured that no slight was intended in any case of non-inclusion

Essentially, this book is an appreciation of the entrepreneurs, the chefs, the managers, the maitre'd's, the hostesses, the kitchen staff, the waiters and the food and beverage suppliers who have all done so much to propel Barbados to its

elevated position as the leading dining destination in the Caribbean. There can be nowhere else in the region where so many good restaurants can be found in such a compact area.

For each restaurant we have attempted to feature the design and ambience; the food; and the chefs and other relevant personalities; as well as supplying one of the chef's favourite recipes.

While providing brief write-ups for each of the restaurants, we have concentrated our emphasis on visual impact with over 350 superb colour photographs. We want this book to be a visual feast that will whet the reader's appetite and inspire continued progress in the ongoing development of restaurants in Barbados and a greater appreciation for the excellent cuisine that they serve.

Best wishes

David Button and Keith Miller

7

Even though Barbados has a well documented international image as an exotic and popular tourist destination which enjoys a level of sophistication not generally associated with the Caribbean, many first time visitors are still taken aback by the surprisingly wide choice and high quality of the fine restaurants found on the island today. Without question, Barbados offers a selection of superb and truly international standard restaurants that is quite disproportionate to its physical status as a remote Caribbean island of a mere 166 square miles. Yet, although it is true that overall standards have increased significantly over the last ten years or so, this phenomenon is not entirely new to Barbados.

From the time of settlement in 1627, the people of Barbados have enjoyed a fine reputation for their inherent ability to successfully host and entertain guests. Even as early as 1657, in his book "A True and Exact History of Barbadoes", Richard Ligon, a visiting Englishman, writes in a state of almost incredulous disbelief about his experience when invited to dinner at a plantation house. He speaks of a huge dining table completely laden down with course after course of as wide a variety of dishes as he has ever seen, and most of which he considers to be "as good as any in the world"; all washed down with a similar selection of excellent spirits and wines. To make his contentment complete, this fine fare was accompanied by "as cheerful a look, and as hearty a welcome, as any man can give to his best friends".

The island's fame as a healthy and hearty destination for rest and recreation seems to have grown even more from this point on. So much so that some 100 years later, when one Lawrence Washington of Virginia, USA, a relatively wealthy and influential man, was looking for a location to try to find a cure for his respiratory illness, of all the places in the world that he could have chosen, he opted to make what was in those days the long and hazardous journey to Barbados. This decision would not necessarily have surprised any knowledgeable person in 1752 since it was widely recognized at that time that Barbados was both an excellent health spa with top class medical care, and a culturally advanced society; notwithstanding the existence of the inhumane, but at that time generally accepted, institution of slavery. What adds spice to Washington's decision to come to Barbados is the fact that he was accompanied by his younger brother George, the future first President of the United States of America. The 19 year-old George Washington learned a great deal during what was his first and only ever journey outside America, and his young mind would have been greatly influenced by what he saw and experienced on the island. We know from his personal diaries, which still exist today, that the young George Washington was hugely impressed by the more convivial aspects of life in Barbados; notably the sumptuous and elegant nature of its dinner parties; exciting cultural events, such as his first ever visit to the theatre; and, last but not least, the beauty and vivacious manner of the ladies. In essence, despite the serious business of being here to accompany his sick brother, young George Washington actually had a good old time in Barbados.

Whereas Washington came to Barbados as an unknown man, long before his days of fame and glory, many, many other world leaders and renowned celebrities have, over the course of the last fifty years in particular, made this relatively tiny island their first choice as a vacation destination; as a location for a second home; or even their permanent place of abode. In the early 1900's a number of wealthy expatriates built holiday homes on the west coast of Barbados, generally lured by the charm of a remote tropical island hideaway which conveniently existed without the discomforts usually associated with such remoteness.

One such devotee of Barbados, the world famous shipping magnate Sir Edward Cunard, who built his home, Glitter Bay, in the area of Porters, was destined by chance to play a pivotal role in the future development of the island's tourism industry. During World War II Sir Edward Cunard was the aide-de-camp to the Governor General in Trinidad, and it was while performing his official duties there that he first met Ronald Tree, who was travelling to the USA as a wartime emissary for Winston Churchill. In conversation, Tree mentioned to Cunard that he was considering buying a piece of land in Trinidad to build a holiday home after the war. Cunard agreed that this was a good idea, but

suggested that Tree visit his home in Barbados, Glitter Bay, before he made his final decision. The offshoot was that Tree did indeed visit Barbados after the war and immediately fell in love with the island. Within a year he bought a piece of land quite close to Glitter Bay and built his magnificent home, Heron Bay, where he was soon entertaining stars of stage and screen, and world leaders of the calibre of Sir Winston Churchill.

So popular was Heron Bay as a tropical escape for this class of visitor that the demand soon outstripped the supply, and the house could no longer accommodate everybody who wished to stay there. This situation opened the eyes of Ronald Tree to the potential for the development of Barbados as an upmarket vacation destination, and so he purchased Sandy Lane, an old sugar estate on the west coast. His dream was fulfilled in 1961 when the international standard Sandy Lane Hotel was first opened, complete with world-class golf course.

The opening of Sandy Lane was the catalyst that sparked the rapid growth of a new, tourism based economy for Barbados; as indeed was the initiative of building a range of luxury villas around the golf course, to be used as a new wave of holiday homes situated off the beach. Throughout the 1970's and 1980's more and more wealthy people wanted to visit Barbados and so, in turn, more and more high-class hotels and villas quickly followed. More recently, the continued success of this sector has encouraged further substantial investment in the 1990's and the early part of the new millennium, which has resulted in Barbados today being home to some of the world's finest hotels and residential communities. The major developments include Royal Westmoreland, a resort community centred around a Robert Trent Jones Jr. championship golf course; Port St. Charles, a beachfront residential community encompassing a modern marina; Sugar Hill, a tennis oriented resort community; Villa Nova, one of the Caribbean's finest plantation great houses which has been transformed into a leading country house hotel; and the new Sandy Lane which, complete with a Tom Fazio championship golf course, has firmly set its sights on being the finest hotel anywhere in the world.

With the advent of these new, world-class properties there obviously came an influx of a new breed of consumer; and, by natural extension, a new level of customer expectations. Generally speaking, the hospitality sector of Barbados has performed well in meeting the difficult challenge of satisfying the extra demands of a more discerning clientele, especially in the areas of restaurants, entertainment, sports and recreational facilities.

Restaurants in Barbados have progressed in leaps and bounds over the last twenty years. In keeping with worldwide modern culinary trends, the wide range of restaurants in Barbados can offer the full gamut of international cuisines - from Caribbean to Mexican; French to Chinese; and Italian to Indian, as well as our own local Bajan dishes and specialities. In fact, even the range of meals that are regularly eaten in family homes throughout Barbados are a clear indication of the many diverse influences that have shaped the kind of food that we eat here today. Over the course of the last four centuries, the Caribbean has been inhabited at various times by people from a broad spectrum of backgrounds and cultures, including Amerindians, Africans, Europeans and Asians.

Thousands of years ago the Caribbean's earliest Amerindian inhabitants, notably the Arawaks and the Caribs after whom the region is named, used to cook their meat and fish on a grill over an open fire. The Arawak word for this style of cooking was "barbacoa", which gradually became 'barbecue' in English. And we still love to barbecue today, as does the rest of the world. The Amerindians also used to preserve their meat in 'casareep', a juice extracted from cassava. Even in this day and age, we still use casareep to preserve the meat used in a popular dish known as "Pepperpot", which is found on menus all around the Caribbean.

The many thousands of Africans who were forcibly shipped to the Caribbean as slaves brought with them their own recipes and methods of preparing food, and they managed to pass on much of this knowledge from generation to generation. Indeed the current national dish of Barbados, 'Cou Cou' served with Flying Fish, is a good example of a Barbadian meal with its culinary roots buried deep in Africa.

The early English settlers of course 'imported' many of their favourite foodstuffs and dishes. To this day Barbadians refer to potatoes as 'English potatoes', as opposed to the local 'sweet potato'. One of the most popular meals in Barbados today is that most English of dishes, 'Roast Beef and Yorkshire Pudding'. 'Macaroni Pie', which is of Italian origin like most pasta dishes, has become part of the staple diet of just about every household in modern Barbados. Other traditionally European dishes have also found their way on to Barbadian menus, becoming accepted over the years as very much part of the local culinary landscape.

The Asian influence in Caribbean cooking has been very significant. Generations of Indian immigrants have bequeathed us the art of a good curry, while Chinese people have taught us how to be more creative with rice and noodles, even establishing 'Chow Mein' as a basic, everyday dish in Barbados.

One of the major reasons for the recent great improvement in the standards of the restaurants in Barbados has been the much improved supply and better quality of ingredients and fresh produce, both local and imported, thus allowing the chefs to introduce a higher level of consistency to their work and allowing them the capacity to be more adventurous.

Another very important factor has been the arrival of international chefs who, in addition to contributing their own creativity to local cuisine, have also been able to pass on their skills and knowledge to Barbadians. In this way our local chefs have been able to learn from their overseas counterparts who have already benefited from the experience of running busy kitchens at the highest level. At the time of writing, the list of chefs working on the island includes people from Barbados, England, Italy, Austria, Germany, USA, Canada, Australia, India, China and the Philippines.

In addition, many of the more enlightened, leading restaurants and hotels in Barbados have had the vision to send their chefs and other staff overseas for further training in specific areas of their trade, as well as to gain the invaluable experience of working in top class establishments in a more developed and more demanding market. In this manner, Barbadians have found themselves working for a period of time in some of the world's most famous restaurants.

The end result of all of these factors combined is that Barbados can today justifiably boast of having a broad range of international quality restaurants that are well able to satisfy both the most demanding of standards and the most whimsical of tastes.

Keith Miller

The Restaurants

bajan blue

In an atmosphere of relaxed elegance, Bajan Blue serves the finest cuisine from the Caribbean and the Mediterranean

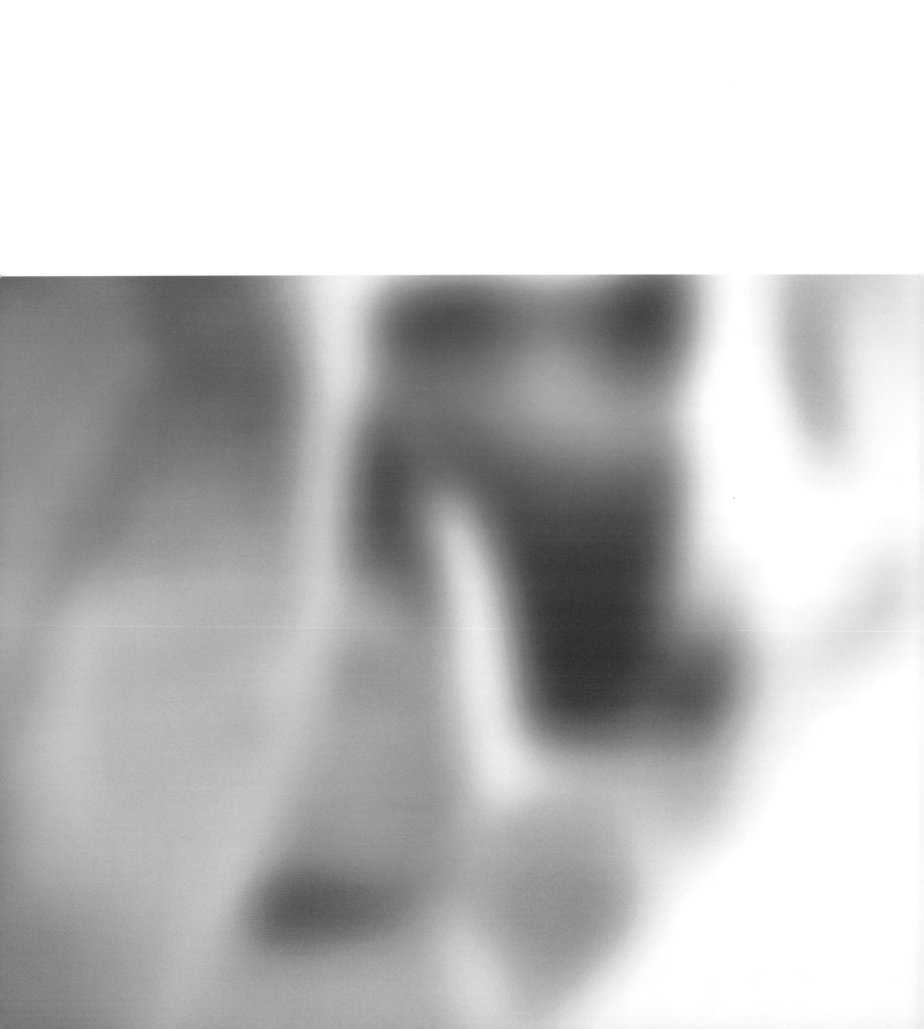

Bajan Blue is the beachside restaurant at the world renowned and lavishly appointed Sandy Lane Hotel. In an atmosphere of relaxed elegance, Bajan Blue serves the finest cuisine from the Caribbean and the Mediterranean, ranging from a lavish, daily breakfast buffet to 'a la carte' lunch and dinner. Offering 'something for everyone', the Bajan Blue culinary team prepares a high quality selection of salads, pizzas, pastas, grilled meats and fresh fish ....from a tuna nicoise salad at lunch to a grilled veal rib chop for dinner. Every Sunday Bajan Blue presents a beautiful lunch buffet with absolutely all the trimmings.

Opposite - Scottish Salmon and Scallop Roulade,
Saffron Potatoes and Watercress Dressing
This page clockwise from top left -
Smoked Salmon and Cream Cheese Gateaux with Beluga Caviar
Asian Sampler Plate with Soy Dressing
Grilled Tiger Shrimp with Asian Slaw and Sweet Chili Mango Salsa

Above - Oven Roasted Tournedos of Venison, Apple, Spinach and Red Cabbage Tian and Red Currant Sauce · Opposite - West Indian Seafood Curry with Lemon Scented Basmati Rice

Opposite - Bitter Chocolate and Raspberry Flower Box with Berry Coulis • Above - Chocolate and Almond Cake with Dried Exotic Fruits

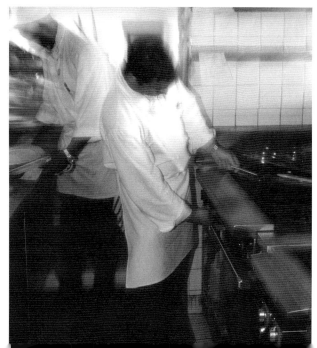

The Executive Sous Chef at Bajan Blue is English born Kelly Jackson. After completing his apprenticeship in England and spending three years at the Holiday Inn in London, Kelly spent a year working aboard the QE2 to expand his practical knowledge before moving to Australia to perfect his trade. Over the course of his five years in Canberra and Melbourne, Kelly won four "Best Restaurant" awards. Prior to accepting his current position at Sandy Lane, Kelly worked in both Nevis and London with the Four Seasons Hotel Group before joining Daphne's Restaurant in London and then arriving in Barbados with the same company.

Kelly's style of cooking has changed over the years, as have peoples' eating expectations. As diners are now more prone to healthier eating, he tries to limit his use of creams, butters and heavy sauces, preferring the lighter Mediterranean way of cooking.

Kelly's favourite two food origins: "Would have to be Italian for its flavour and Japanese for its freshness. In fact the restaurant overseas that I most visit is Nobu in London. For me cooking is a passion. I think that a lot of chefs eat with their eyes, meaning that when you go out to dine, you are presented with a beautiful decorative plate of food, but the tastes are just not there! I don't want to just present a pretty picture. When you leave my restaurant I want you to still have sensational flavours creating in your mouth."

Herb-Crusted Rack of Lamb with Courgettes, Fava Beans & Pancetta

Ingredients

1 Rack of Lamb
1 tsps Dijon Mustard
1 oz Pancetta
1 Artichoke
2 oz Courgette
1 oz Fava Beans
2 Mint Leaves
3 oz Veal Stock
Salt & Pepper

For the Herb Crust
3 oz Ciabatta
1 oz Lemon Rind
1 oz Capers
1 oz Anchovies
1 oz Chopped Onions
1 oz Pitted Black Olives
3 oz Parsley
3 oz Basil

Method

To make the herb crust, preheat the oven to 120C. Lay the ciabatta, lemon rind, capers, anchovies, onions and olives on a baking sheet and dry out for 2 hours.

Transfer the dried ingredients to a food processor and blend with the basil and parsley, until a fine grain breadcrumb appears.

Seal the rack of lamb in a pan to retain all the juices for 2-3 minutes, then brush the lamb with mustard and roll into the fine herb crust until completely covered. Bake the lamb in the oven for approximately 8 minutes or until your desired cooking degree.

Whilst the lamb is cooking, warm a fry pan and add the strips of pancetta and wedges of artichoke. Season well.

Stir in the courgettes, fava beans and mint, and then add a little veal stock to bind the mixture together.

To serve, cut the lamb rack into cutlets, arrange over the courgette mixture and drizzle remaining veal stock around the plate.

calabaza

An impressive waterfall, cascading dramatically down a wall at the entrance into the restaurant, provides an immediate hint that something different and out of the ordinary for Barbados awaits around the corner .... and so it does.

First opened in December 2001 by owner Allan Evelyn, Calabaza is an attractive restaurant which successfully combines good food, a classic cliff top location overlooking the sea, and some very interesting architecture and design.

An impressive waterfall, cascading dramatically down a wall at the entrance into the restaurant, provides an immediate hint that something different and out of the ordinary for Barbados awaits around the corner .... and so it does. Neatly layered in a series of gently descending decks, the overall theme of Calabaza reflects a Moroccan influence, with warm sand and terra cotta colours and a touch of Mediterranean blue, all creating a relaxed and cosy mood which is further enhanced by lanterns and creative soft lighting.

The General Manager, the ever popular Peter Harris who has established himself over the years as the island's best known bar and restaurant manager, is devoted to making sure that everybody enjoys Calabaza to the maximum and has a wonderful, complete dining experience. Peter and his efficient and friendly team are on hand to welcome their guests, who can choose to linger at the Bar & Lounge on the first deck or go directly to their table on the dining terrace at the water's edge.

Opposite - Roasted Scallops with Crushed Tomatoes, Seaweed Salad and Asian Vinaigrette

Above left - Fillet of Pork with Chorizo Sausage Bubble & Squeak, Glazed Carrots, Madeira Mustard Seed Jus

Above middle - Charcoal Grilled Half Lobster with Garlic & Chive Butter served with a Garden Salad

Above right - Miso Rubbed Chicken Breast stuffed with Plantain served with Tempura Sweet Potato with Mandarin, Sake & Chili Vinaigrette

Above - Seared Salmon with a Raspberry Crème Fraiche with a Marche Salad
Opposite - Peppered Tuna served rare with Eggplant Caviar, French Lentils in a Veal Stock Reduction

Opposite - Double Espresso – Smooth Dark & White Chocolate Mousse presented in Tuile Cups with Chocolate Shavings

Above - Baked Lemon & Lime Tart garnished with Fruit Salsa and Cardamom Syrup

The Chef at Calabaza is British born Stephen Bredemear, who was trained in France under Laurent Ferre, the Sous Chef to the late, famous Chef Alain Chapel, at the three-star Michelin Mionnay Lyon. In addition to a spell in Bermuda at the Once Upon A Table restaurant, Stephen has also worked at several top class British hotels, including the world famous, exclusive Chewton Glen Hotel, which was awarded five Relais & Chateaux red stars and one Michelin star.

The Chef, whose own personal favourite choice of restaurants are the Alain Ducasse Restaurant in Monte Carlo and Marco Pierre White in London, describes his style of cooking as: "Modern contemporary food. I was definitely influenced by my time spent in France, but I also like the crossover style of cooking which is so popular at the moment. Food should be kept simple and uncomplicated. A proper balance has to be obtained between the ingredients so that, once the dish is properly prepared, it will be enjoyed."

Crispy Wok-Seared Snapper with Stir-Fried Vegetables and Dipping Sauce

Ingredients

Red Snapper
Bok Choy
Red and green peppers
Bean sprouts

Method

Season the snapper fillet in flour and cornstarch mixture. Cook the snapper in olive oil and sesame oil. For the stir-fried vegetables, lightly blanch the bok choy, carrots, peppers and bean sprouts, then stir-fry them in sesame oil and oyster sauce.

To serve, place the vegetables on a plate, and put the fish on top of the vegetables. Drizzle with basil oil, beet oil and ginger oil. Serve the dipping sauce on the side.

To prepare the Dipping Sauce - add red onions, garlic, ginger, sweet chili sauce, fish sauce, rice vinegar and sugar to water. Bring to a boil, then add chopped herbs.

carambola

Every table at Carambola enjoys a prime spot along the edge of the cliff, with some of them neatly tucked away for greater privacy, and the whole restaurant backs onto a beautifully landscaped garden with lots of mature trees, which is quite rare for such a seaside location.

It really would be hard to find a restaurant with a more beautiful coastal setting than Carambola. The view from the restaurant's main dining terrace, which is dramatically perched along the edge of a 300 foot wide coral cliff and overlooks the tranquil waters of the west coast, is truly captivating: both by day when the sea glitters in an incredible variety of aquamarines and blues; and by night when clever, soft lighting creates a romantic atmosphere and at the same time illuminates the sea ...... just enough to make it possible to see passing fish and the resident group of Stingrays as they make their regular visit each evening!

Every table at Carambola enjoys a prime spot along the edge of the cliff, with some of them neatly tucked away for greater privacy, and the whole restaurant backs onto a beautifully landscaped garden with lots of mature trees, which is quite rare for such a seaside location.

Carambola, which is named after the fruit of the same name growing on a tree close to the restaurant's entrance, is the brainchild of its owner, Robin Walcott, a very successful Barbadian entrepreneur. Incidentally, the presence of the Stingrays can also be attributed to Robin since he just about guarantees their appearance by wading into the sea himself every evening at 7:00 pm to feed them!

Robin opened Carambola in 1987 with the aim of creating a more casual type of restaurant with an emphasis on a quality all-round experience – good food and efficient service, provided in an ambience of relaxed, Caribbean comfort. The Carambola philosophy is to give people maximum dining pleasure by encouraging them to slow down enough to fully enjoy the food and the surroundings .... take in the gardens, listen to the waves, watch the Stingrays, look for turtles, relax.

Opposite - Vietnamese Style Lobster & Snow Crab Spring Rolls with Sweet & Hot Sauce • Above - Atlantic Salmon Garlic Lemon on a Bed of Pasta

Previous page left - Spiced Chicken with Tamarind & Ginger Coating on White Rice
Previous page right - Grilled Caribbean Lobster served with Crunchy Asian Vegetables & Wild Rice
Opposite - Red Barbequed Pork with Fluffy White Rice & Tangy Fruit Sauce • Above - Chargrilled Mahi Mahi with Spicy Bell Pepper Salsa

Some 16 years after opening, the mood at Carambola is still pleasantly 'at ease', but the menu has today evolved into a more sophisticated selection, with a high standard of preparation. Carambola's team of skilled Barbadian chefs are especially adept at creating excellent seafood dishes, often serving delicious varieties of local fish not frequently seen on the average restaurant menu, accompanied by the freshest and best quality local vegetables. Carambola's cuisine also reflects a hint of Asian influence, which is a direct result of Robin Walcott's own gastronomic travel experiences in the Far East. To complement the varied nature of the menu, Carambola's wine list features a wide choice of wines taken from outside the mainstream brands and countries of origin.

Spiced Chicken
Serves 4

Ingredients

4 plump chicken breasts

For the Marinade
Olive Oil
White wine
Garlic
Coriander
Parsley
Chives
Eastern spicy chili sauce

Method

Chop and mix all the ingredients for the marinade in a saucepan. Reduce the mixture on a low heat and put to one side.

Place the chicken breasts in the marinade and leave for at least a couple of hours. It is best to cut slits in the skin first to absorb the marinade.

When ready, pat the chicken breasts dry and place them on a hot grill for a couple of minutes, with the skin-side down first. Hold them down with a spatula. There will be much spitting and smoke, but don't worry - this is what you want. When golden brown, turn the chicken breasts over and cook on the other side for about five minutes. You can spoon on a little of the marinade if you like to keep the chicken moist and add more flavour.

When the chicken breasts are cooked, take them off the grill and put them on a baking tray. Lightly sprinkle breadcrumbs over the chicken and then pour the remaining marinade over it. Place the chicken breasts in a hot oven for a further ten minutes.

Serve with a fruity sauce, such as mango, which we use because it is readily available.

We have not specified amounts. Try not to be too scientific. You can never reproduce what you eat in restaurants. Choose your amounts according to your own taste and those of your guests.

Remember good food is about having fun. Good luck.

champers

Champers is a very popular restaurant and wine bar which has fully earned its widespread reputation for consistently producing good quality food.

Located in Worthing on the south coast of the island, Champers is a very popular restaurant and wine bar which has fully earned its widespread reputation for consistently producing good quality food and giving excellent value for money. First opened in 1995 by Owner/Manager Chiryl Newman, Champers is situated right on the water's edge and opens out onto the sea, giving rise to a pleasantly breezy dining environment and spectacular views. Chiryl is herself a very popular and fun-loving person, so it is a natural extension that the atmosphere at Champers tends to be happy and informal, and the staff friendly and helpful. Downstairs is more of a busy bar, whilst upstairs represents a more traditional dining area. In both cases patrons are offered an extensive wine list and a full range of cocktails.

Chiryl works with a team of chefs to produce a very varied menu which though it features lots of seafood also offers a tempting array of meat dishes. Champers wants to provide "something to suit every palate".

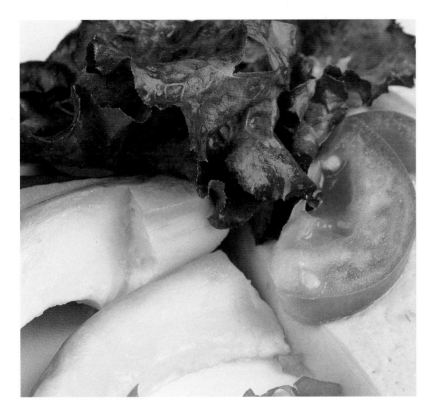

Opposite - Shrimp & Mango Vinaigrette Salad
Above left - Smoked Salmon Terrine with Avocado and Caper Dressing
Above right - Baked Potato with Scottish Smoked Salmon & Sour Cream

Above · Caribbean Shrimp Curry with Poppadom & Steamed Vegetables · Opposite · Champers Very Special Smoked Salmon Sandwich
Following pages: Left · Pan Fried Red Snapper with a Mango & Pepper Salsa · Right · White Chocolate Cheesecake with a Strawberry Coulis

The Barbadian Head Chef, David Jordan, who particularly enjoys working with local ingredients, first trained and worked here in Barbados before expanding his knowledge and experience by accepting positions in Tortola, BVI, and in New York. A solid, family man, David is best motivated by hard work and a busy restaurant. He enjoys the working atmosphere at Champers where he says "all of the staff are like a family".

The Champers policy is simply "To serve the best food possible at the best price possible; and to try to give value for money whilst producing excellent quality and service". It is a fundamental principal that keeps both visitors and locals coming back for more.

Champers Shrimp and Mango Salad
Serves 2

Ingredients - Mango Vinaigrette
1 ripe mango peeled and removed from
the seed
1 cup of white wine vinegar
1 cup olive oil
1 tbsp honey
Salt and pepper to taste
4 sprigs of parsley

Ingredients - Salad
8 large peeled and cooked shrimp
2 lettuce cups and shredded lettuce
(made from iceberg lettuce)
1 large ripe but firm mango sliced
Julienne of red and green sweet peppers
2 sprigs of parsley

Method - Mango Vinaigrette
Place all ingredients except parsley in a blender
and blend until smooth, and yellow in colour; add
parsley and then blend until parsley is chopped in to
small pieces but is still visible.
Refrigerate the vinaigrette until needed. It can
actually be made the day before.

Method - Salad
Place a lettuce cup filled with shredded lettuce in the
centre of a plate, and arrange the mango slices
around it. Place 4 shrimp in each cup and top with
mango vinaigrette. Garnish with julienne peppers
and parsley.

daphne's

This chic and glamorous restaurant serves a menu which has been inspired by the classic Italian style of living and eating, but reinvented for contemporary tastes and healthy lifestyle needs. Each dish is beautifully simple in its conception, with the focus on fresh, quality ingredients, with inspired flavours.

The renowned London-based restaurant, Daphne's, can now also be found in the heart of the west coast of Barbados. Situated right on the water's edge, Daphne's offers a metropolitan and cross-cultural dining experience rarely found in this part of the world. Though the restaurant has its feet quite literally in the Caribbean Sea, it is decorated in the same minimalist, state-of-the-art style popular these days in London or New York. This chic and glamorous restaurant serves a menu which has been inspired by the classic Italian style of living and eating, but reinvented for contemporary tastes and healthy lifestyle needs. Each dish is beautifully simple in its conception, with the focus on fresh, quality ingredients, with inspired flavours.

The wine list at Daphne's deserves a special mention, since excellent wines have been carefully selected from top producers in Italy, France and other regions of the world. The attractive sunken cocktail bar, featuring delicious exotic cocktails and Martinis, is another highlight at Daphne's.

Above - San Danielle with Zucchini, Sun-Dried Tomato and Montassio Cheese

Left - Local Mozzerella with Tomatoes and Basil Oil

Above - Pear and Endive Salad with Pecorino Cheese
Opposite - Seafood Salad – Mussels, Clams, Fresh Water Prawns and Seared Tuna with Parsley and Caper Salsa

Previous page left - Grilled Local Fish with Green Beans and Tomato Salsa
Previous page right - Seared Tuna Salad with Sweet Mustard Dressing
Opposite - "Tiramisu" A True Italian Classic Made with Mascaponi and Coffee Sauce

The chef at Daphne's is Nick Bell, an Englishman. Nick started work at the Savoy in 1988 and after completing his training he moved on to work at some of London's top restaurants, including The Capital Hotel, The Canteen, Gidleigh Park and Cecconis. For the last four years he trained under and ran the kitchen at Zafferano Restaurant with Giorgio Locatelli; during this time Zafferano was voted best Italian Restaurant in London for three consecutive years and was awarded a Michelin Star.

Nick loves Italian food and wine in general, but especially from the Tuscany and Lombardy regions. While on holiday in Italy recently he discovered a restaurant called L'Arogosta, The Lobster, which he thought was fantastic and yet so simple - something which is very close to Nick's own culinary philosophy. He admires "Food that is not passed through twenty pairs of hands to reach the plate; made with the best and freshest ingredients. and simply prepared."

Tuna Salad with Pickled Cucumber and Mustard Dressing
Serves 4

Ingredients
250g Tuna loin cut into 1inch squares
1 local cucumber
100g spinach
50ml mustard dressing
rock salt

Pickle for the cucumbers
50ml water
50ml white wine vinegar
50ml sugar

Mustard Dressing
200ml white wine vinegar
1 tablespoon American mustard
600ml Olive oil

Method
With this recipe you have to do a little preparation first.

1. Boil the ingredients for the pickle and allow to cool.
2. Make the dressing by gently adding the vinegar to the mustard and then slowly adding the olive oil.
3. Slice the cucumber
4. Trim the tuna into 1 Inch square loins.
5. Pick and wash the spinach

To sear the tuna you have to warm a non-stick frying pan and a little oil.
While the pan is heating, season the tuna generously with cracked black pepper and sea salt. By the time you have finished, the pan will be hot and ready to sear the tuna for 30 seconds on all four sides. Remove from the pan and cool. Slice the tuna, gaining 7 to 8 slices from each loin, and pour the pickle over the cucumbers.

To assemble the salad, mix the spinach leaves with the mustard dressing and place in the middle of the plate, then place a slice of tuna and a slice of pickled cucumber alternatively around the spinach. Season and add a little more dressing around the side.

emerald palm

Emerald Palm is a casually elegant, family owned restaurant housed in a warm and friendly, coral stone country-home. The restaurant enjoys a very relaxed and happy ambience for dining, both inside and out.

Above - Grilled Yellow Fin Tuna Coriander Risotto, Stir-fry Exotic
Vegetables, soya and herb jus

First opened in 1997 and conveniently located on the inland side of the main west coast road, Emerald Palm is a casually elegant, family owned restaurant housed in a warm and friendly coral stone country home. Opening out onto surrounding beautifully landscaped gardens, the restaurant enjoys a very relaxed and happy ambience for dining, both inside and out.

Brian Tatem is the restaurant manager and, with his many years of experience in the hospitality business and a natural love for good food, he and his energetic team will do all in their power to ensure that each of their guests leave Emerald Palm with a great sense of satisfaction.

Previous page left - Caesar Salad with Jumbo Shrimp and Marinated Chicken Breast
Previous page right - Local Chicken Breast, Stuffed with Herbs, Scallop Potatoes, Balsamic Jus
Above - Sultana and Citron Flavoured Bread & Butter Pudding, Glazed Apples, Toffee Sauce
Opposite - Classic Crème Caramel, Coffee Anglaise, Caramelized Local Bananas

Describing their style as "a modern approach to international cuisine", the highly trained chefs at Emerald Palm are committed to offering only the freshest and best quality local fish, island vegetables and fresh herbs, as well as using the finest imported ingredients such as top grade, aged, corn-fed beef. The wide and varied menu provides diners with an appealing, manageable range of dishes.

The good food at Emerald Palm is complemented by a broad selection of distinctive new world wines and a fully stocked bar, which also serves as an ideal afternoon 'hang out' for some quality 'R&R'.

Grilled Marinated Shrimp in Soya and Ginger, with Vegetable Ribbons, Sweet and Sour Sauce

Ingredients:

6 jumbo shrimps
Red, yellow, green, sweet peppers
Onion, chives, mushrooms, garlic, carrots and zucchini
1 cup of ginger
1/2 cup soya sauce
1/2 cup of vinegar
1 chopped tomato
1 cup sugar
1/2 cup tomato juice
1 clove of garlic
Salt and black pepper

Method:

Cut into ribbons the red, yellow and green, sweet peppers, the onions, chives, mushrooms, garlic, carrots and zucchini. Then stir-fry it all in soya sauce.

To prepare the sweet and sour sauce: Mix 1 cup of ginger, 1/2 cup soya sauce, 1/2 cup of vinegar, 1 chopped tomato, 1 cup sugar, 1/2 teaspoon salt, black pepper to taste, 1/2 cup tomato juice, 1 onion and 1 clove of garlic. Bring the mixture to a boil, set aside to cool, then blend until all the ingredients are fully pureed.

Peel and clean 6 jumbo shrimp, marinate in 1/2 cup soya sauce and 1/2 cup of ginger. Saute the shrimps for a minute or two. Do not overcook.

To Serve:

Place the stir-fry onto a 12-inch plate, place the shrimps on the stir-fry and drizzle with the sweet and sour sauce.

patisserie & bistro flindt

Quite unique in Barbados as the island's only truly authentic patisserie.

Owned and energetically managed by Carsten Flindt and his wife Zoe - both Barbadian by birth - Patisserie Flindt first opened its doors in August 1998 in Holetown. Quite unique in Barbados, as the island's only truly authentic patisserie, Flindt's produces a really phenomenal range of goods including breads, breakfast pastries, a whole range of delicious canapés, sandwiches, pies, quiche, pate, salads, home-made fresh cream ganache chocolates, gift ideas, bottled oils and sauces, individual desserts for home entertaining, elaborate chocolate cakes and other amazing creations, as well as a selection of delicious picnic baskets. Visitors to Flindt's are always blown away by Carsten's outstanding chocolate and sugar sculptures.

In 2000 Carsten and Zoe opened a second Patisserie Flindt outlet on the South Coast. However these premises quickly proved to be too small for the increased demand and so, in May 2002, they jumped at an opportunity to move to another location just a few doors down with more space and a much better setting. At this time the decision was taken to expand their name to Patisserie & Bistro Flindt, and start serving genuine "Bistro" fare for lunch and dinner, as well as "Cooked Breakfast" at the weekends. With a mission statement that promises "Quality Product, Quality Service - a Total Quality Experience", Carsten and Zoe work continuously to ensure consistency, a quality that they consider vital in their business.

Opposite - Rustic Artisan Breads • Above left - Flindt's Weekend Breakfast • Above Right - Mixed Seafood with Puff Pastry Crown

Top - Oven Roasted Thin Crust Pizza - A House Speciality

Above - Oven Roasted North Atlantic Salmon, glazed with Maple Syrup served with Spicy Asian Noodles and Pan Fried Vegetables

Opposite - Canapés: Chicken & Basil in Filo; Smoked Salmon, New Potato and Sour Cream Chive; Tuna Tartare in Barquette

Above - Deluxe Colenso Cake · Opposite - Kiwi and Mandarin Fruit Tart

At age 16 Carsten Flindt joined the Savoy hotel as an apprentice under Barry Colenso, Executive Pastry Chef, and Anton Edelmann, Executive Chef. He stayed there for 3 years and gained a wealth of knowledge. After gaining further valuable job experience serving on a cruise line and doing a few stints in London, Carsten returned to Barbados on a permanent basis in 1992; working at Carambola, The Cliff, The Sandpiper and Coral Reef, before setting up his own business with his wife Zoe.

Carsten took part in a number of culinary industry competitions while training at the Savoy; and in 1996 he participated in the Caribbean Regional Culinary competition, winning the individual Gold Award for 'Best Pastry Chef in the Caribbean', as well as a Team Gold Award with the rest of the Barbados team.

Carsten Flindt describes his style as being: "Taking little bits from everyone, putting in my own thoughts and ideas, tweaking things a bit more and hey presto - you've got something new!"

Flindt's Fruit Tart

Equipment:
1 – 12" Fluted tart ring with removable base

Sweet Pastry Ingredients:
1lb 2oz flour
12oz butter
2 eggs
4oz sugar

Custard Filling Ingredients:
2pts milk
8oz sugar
8 egg yolks
1/2 tsp. vanilla essence
4 oz flour

Sweet Pastry Method:
In a small electric mixer cream the butter and sugar till soft and fluffy. Incorporate the flour with the egg. Rest in the fridge for 1 hour.
Remove pastry from the fridge and roll out to a 1/2 cm thickness and line a 12" ring. Ensure that the pastry is rolled out enough so you have an over hang.
Bake the shell blind by placing parchment paper or greaseproof paper in the shell and filling with rice so as to stop the pastry from rising.
Cook for 25 to 30 minutes at 350° till light and golden brown. Put aside to cool.

Custard Filling Method:
Place the milk and vanilla to boil on the stove.
Place the flour, yolks and sugar in a metal bowl and whisk until you have a smooth consistency.
When the milk has boiled pour it into your yolk mixture and gently whisk till the mixture is incorporated properly.
Pour the mixture back into the pot you boiled the milk in and keep cooking on a medium flame till the custard starts to thicken. Put aside and cool.
When the shell has cooled fill it with the custard and decorate with fruits to your liking.

josef's

Josef's Restaurant is a beautifully restored Barbadian home sitting on a cliff edge overlooking the sea, just a mere few feet above the waves.

Located in the famous St. Lawrence Gap on the South Coast of Barbados, Josef's Restaurant is a beautifully restored Barbadian home sitting on a cliff edge overlooking the sea, just a mere few feet above the waves. The restaurant was established by the renowned Chef Josef Schwaiger some twelve years ago and is regarded as one of the finest dining experiences in Barbados. Chef/Patron Thomas Harris has created a menu with a fusion of European, Thai, Caribbean and Asian flavours, specializing in seafood and haute cuisine. The architectural design of the restaurant, with its cliff side setting offers the diner an unforgettable experience. Josef's restaurant is also a perfect venue for weddings and special functions with its well-manicured gardens and gazebos set on the edge of the cliff.

Previous page right - Grilled Caribbean Rock Lobster with Pernod Beurre Blanc Sauce

Previous page left - Sushi & Sashimi, Mackie Roll, Salmon, Tuna, Shrimp, Dorado, Wasabi and Pickled Ginger

Opposite - Calamato & Olive Crusted Dorado with a Pink Peppercorn Sauce

This page top - Sea Salt Crusted Duck Breast, Seared Spinach, Sweet Potato Mash, Balsamic Reduction with Rasberry Coulis

This page bottom - Spicy Crab Cake with Mango & Avocado Salsa, Saffron & Thai Chilli Sauce

Chef/Patron Thomas Harris, MHCIMA, and Chef De Cuisine Charmaine Maynard have together successfully 'brought the west coast to the south'. Charmaine has gained a wealth of experience from some of the top restaurants on the west coast, including the famous Sandy Lane, Carambola and Mullins. She has been awarded a silver and bronze medal in recently held culinary competitions and now ranks as one of the top female Head Chefs in the Caribbean. Thomas Harris has spent much of his working career in England. A perfectionist who will not tolerate anything less than the 'Best in Good Food, Good Drink and Good Service', Thomas specializes in Asian, Middle-Eastern and Caribbean cooking. His own personal favourite meal is "A spicy bowl of New Orleans Seafood Gumbo with a bottle of one of Australia's finest New World wines such as Hunter Valley Hope Estate Chardonnay".

Thomas maintains that "If at the end of your meal you have a gastronomic orgasm, then you have had good food."

Olive and Herb Crusted Dorado served with Creamed Truffle Potatoes, Sautéed Vegetables, Pink Peppercorn, Saffron and Cilantro Sauce
Serves 6

Olive and Herb Crust Ingredients:
6 oz freshly grated Parmesan Cheese
6 oz freshly chopped herbs (cilantro, dill, parsley & basil)
4 oz Black Olives (Green Olives optional)
1lb creamed New Potatoes
1/4 tsp finely ground peppercorns
2 tbsp chopped shallots

Pink Peppercorn Sauce Ingredients:
4 oz Pink peppercorns
4 oz shallots
2 oz white cooking wine
2 tbsp unsalted butter
Salt and pepper to taste
1/2 litre cooking cream
1/2 litre fish stock
Pinch of saffron
2 oz olive oil

Fish Preparation Ingredients:
(for a single serving)
6-8 oz fillet of Mahi Mahi
Juice of one lime
Crushed sea salt
1 oz olive oil
2 oz herbed breadcrumbs

Olive and Herb Crust Method:
Combine the Parmesan cheese, black olives, fresh herbs and black pepper corns in a kitchen blender. Roughly grind but do not puree. Remove mixture and combine in a bowl with the creamed potatoes. Place mixture on wax paper and roll into a log, twisting both ends of the wax paper to get a log roughly two inches in diameter. Place in freezer for minimum 1-2 hours before required.

Pink Peppercorn Sauce Method:
In a saucepan heat the olive oil and add the unsalted butter. Add the shallots and sweat them. Add a very small pinch of saffron to allow the aroma of the saffron to infuse quickly. Add the white wine and cook for a further 2-3 minutes on medium heat. Add the fish stock cook a further 2 to 3 minutes. Lower the heat to a simmer and add the cooking cream. Cook on low heat for 20 minutes till the saffron adds a light yellow tint to the sauce. To serve the sauce, get a separate saucepan, spoon out 6-8 oz of the prepared sauce, add a teaspoon of pink peppercorns and heat till the flavour of the pink peppercorns infuse while steering the sauce, do not bring it to a boil to avoid splitting.

Fish Preparation Method: (for a single serving)
Place the filleted fish in the mixture of olive oil, lime juice and sea salt. Remove and place in the breadcrumb mixture until all sides are coated. In a frying pan heat olive oil and fry the fish to brown all sides, do not cook the fish at this point. Remove from the frying pan and place it on a small baking pan. Place two slices of the prepared herb crust covering one side of the fish. Complete the cooking of the fish with the herb crust in a convection oven or regular oven. Depending on the cut of the fillet and it's thickness the cooking time can vary from 5-8 minutes. Be careful not to over cook the fish as this would make it dry. Remove the fish when cooked, this can be determined by gently pressing the fish to check for a "soft firmness". The crust should be browned slightly but not burned. Place the fish on the truffle-creamed potatoes (one teaspoon of truffle oil to 2lbs of creamed potatoes) seasonal sautéed vegetables and encircle the fish with the pink peppercorns and saffron sauce, garnish with deep fried basil and serve.

la bella collina

The outstanding view from the poolside terrace, overlooking the beautifully landscaped surroundings and the Caribbean Sea, is in complete harmony with the quality of the food and the service provided.

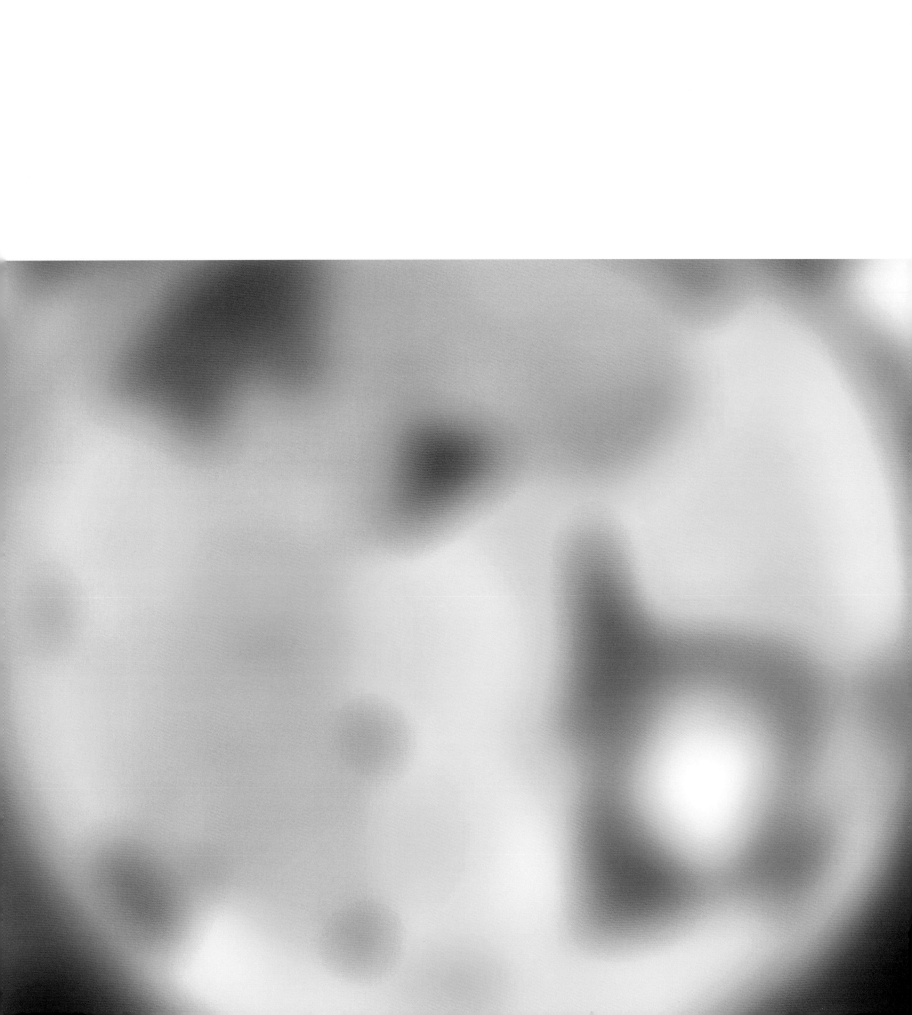

Open since January 2002 and located in the elegantly designed Club House at David Lloyd's Sugar Hill Resort, La Bella Collina is a welcome addition to the fine restaurants on the West Coast. The outstanding view from the poolside terrace, overlooking the beautifully landscaped surroundings and the Caribbean Sea, is in complete harmony with the quality of the food and the service provided. Chef Franco Parisi and the well-trained staff offer a delightful taste of Mediterranean cuisine, accompanied by an interesting selection of specially imported Italian, French and New World Wines.

Opposite - Red Snapper with Potato & Dill Tart, Leeks & Saffron Sauce
Above - Roast Saddle of Lamb, Pan Fried Polenta, Fried Zucchini & Garlic Rosemary

Above · Gratin Goat Cheese with Grilled Vegetable & Red Pepper Sauce · Opposite · Tagliolini with Sea Scallops & Shell Fish & Caviar

Previous page left - Mixed Seafood Plate in Chilli Garlic & White Wine Sauce
Previous page right - Saffron & Quail Risotto in Parmesan Basket Twill
Opposite - Chargrilled Squid with Celery & Pepper Salad in Black Ink Sauce
Above - Tiramisu with Caramel & Chocolate Garnish in Biscuit Basket

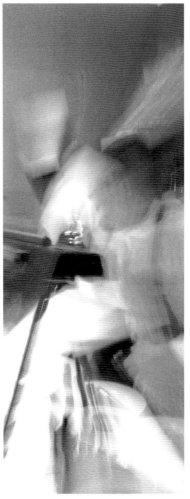

Prior to coming to Barbados, Chef Franco Parisi, from Varese in Italy, has worked for the last 12 years all around the world in some of the most successful restaurants awarded stars by Michelin, Zagat and Carlton. His simple philosophy as a chef is that "Providing great food, excellent service and good value for money is the key to a successful restaurant".

At La Bella Collina, correct cooking techniques and timing are always considered very important basic elements, and it is this solid foundation that then enables Franco's passion and sense of perfection to come to the fore and successfully produce such flavoursome food. All of the pastas, bread, ice creams and sorbets are home-made, and presented in a traditional yet creative way.

Franco says "I like to think of myself as a Maestro Del Risotto's, a master of risottos, because it's one of those dishes that needs extra passion and passion is what I exude most".

One of the chef's favourite places to eat abroad is Nobu, "Because you just can't beat the simplicity of the food".

Quail and Saffron Risotto
Serves 4

Ingredients:
500 gr. Arborio or Cannaroli Rice
1 small onion
1 gr. natural Saffron or 2 bags of Saffron
Powder
4 Quails
1 lt. chicken or vegetable stock
100 gr. Grated Parmesan
80 gr. Butter
100 ml. White Wine
50 ml. Olive Oil

Method:
    Place the quails in boiling stock for twenty minutes, remove the quail and let them cool for a few minutes. De-bone the quail with a fork.
    Braise the onion in olive oil with the quail meat on a low heat. Once it starts to get a golden brown, add the rice and the wine. This process is called 'toasting the grain of the rice'. Once the wine is completely evaporated, add the saffron and the stock. The stock should be added with a ladle slowly for about twenty minutes. Mix the rice every few minutes to avoid it sticking to the pan. Once the grain inside of the rice has completely disappeared, turn off the heat. Add the Parmesan and butter. Mix and serve.

la mer

While La Mer's attractive water's edge location and its accompanying nautical themed decor undeniably create an outstanding ambience, it is the excellent food that makes a visit to this restaurant so richly enjoyable and truly memorable.

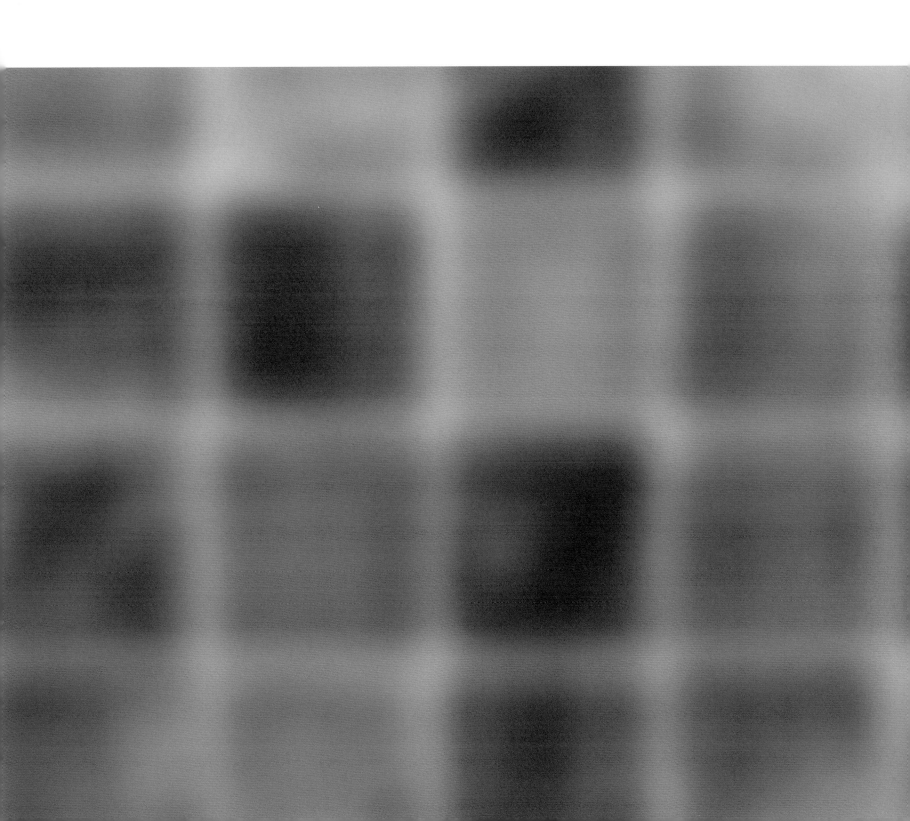

The picturesque location of La Mer, on the very edge of the marina at Port St. Charles on the island's west coast, offers a dining setting which is quite unique in Barbados, and one which very much matches up to the highest standards of even the most discerning of restaurant 'fanatics'. For an especially rewarding and pleasantly decadent experience, it is even possible to sail to Port St. Charles, moor alongside the restaurant, simply step ashore and sit down at your table. However, while La Mer's attractive water's edge location and its accompanying nautical themed decor undeniably create an outstanding ambience, it is the excellent food that makes a visit to this restaurant so richly enjoyable and truly memorable.

Above · Chargrilled Flatbread with Roasted Vegetables · Opposite · Canapés at La Mer Bar

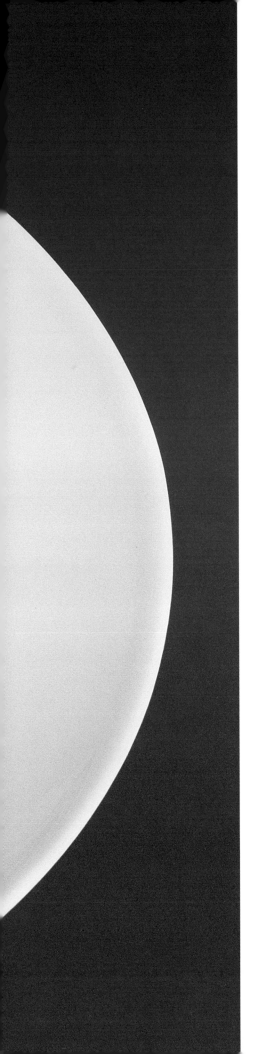

Opposite - Lobster & Baby Vegetable 'Pot au Feu'
Above - Grilled Vegetable Terrine with Fresh Goats Cheese

Above · Sugar Dome of Rum and White Chocolate Pudding Caramelised Banana · Opposite · Mango Bruleé

By the age of 25, La Mer's Chef/Owner, Germany-born Master Chef Hans Schweitzer, had gained the distinguished title of Maitre de Cuisine from Heidelberg Hotel School. His illustrious career then saw him acquiring an incredible range of experience and skills, working and training in many different facets of cuisine in as diverse places as Iran, Belgium and England, before he ultimately opened several successful restaurants of his own. Hans first came to Barbados to work with the Hilton and since then he has been associated with several of the island's leading hotels and restaurants, notably Sandy Lane where he served as Executive Chef for several years.

In keeping with Han's varied experiences and multi-faceted talents, the menu at La Mer offers a wide range of choices, covering an eclectic selection of contemporary dishes.

Reflecting on his career Hans notes that, "I went through many phases, from artistic work to fine saucier. I was very inspired by the French Michelin Star chefs with their beautiful silky sauces and stocks; but I also enjoyed working with specialty buffets where you could actually excel at showpieces."

Mango Brulée
Serves 6

Ingredients
Six 3" Ramekins
1 Split Vanilla Bean
2 Ripe Mangoes
7 Egg Yolks
1/2 ltr Cream
75 gms White Sugar
1 Tbsp Rum
Icing Sugar to dust

Method
   Preheat oven to 160 C. Peel the mangoes, then cut four even slices for each brulée and put to one side. Cut off all remaining mango and put into a blender; blend to a smooth purée. Bring the cream and split vanilla bean to boil. Whisk the egg yolk, sugar and rum to a smooth creamy mixture. Pour in boiling cream and whisk swiftly. Add the mango purée and stir. Sieve the mixture through a fine sieve and divide into the six ramekins. Cook slowly for 30 minutes. Take out of the oven. The brulées should be firm and set but should still have a little wobble within!! Leave to cool for twenty minutes. Then place into a fridge and cool for several hours.
   Sprinkle the mango slices with sugar and caramelise under a hot grill or with a blow torch. When ready to serve, add the caramelised mango slices to the brulée. Dust with icing sugar.

la terra

From the moment that you first make your way up the stone staircase leading into "La Terra", you know that you are entering a welcoming world of understated elegance .

From the moment that you first make your way up the stone staircase leading into "La Terra", you know that you are entering a welcoming world of understated elegance - a world where the classic Caribbean scenario of softly lit palm trees swaying against a backdrop of the moonlit sea has been cleverly infused with an atmosphere of Tuscan romance. The soft, golden glow of La terra is further enhanced by the use of a blend of pale, earthy tones; the simple beauty of modern furniture; subtle, shaded lighting; and the occasional ebb and flow of gently billowing curtains.

Previous page left - Carpaccio of Beef with Rocket Leaves & Parmesan Shavings
Previous page right - Littleneck Clams tossed with Fettuccine, Garlic, Chilli & Herbs
Above - Oven Roasted Quail with Foie Gras, Couscous & Pine Nuts
Opposite - Seared Sesame Seed Tuna Salad

Opposite - Potato Gnocchi with ' Jerked' Pork on a Sweet Pea Pureé

Above - Grilled Barracuda on Grilled Mediterrean Vegetables with Capers & Aioli

Above - Banana & Coconut Bread Pudding on Chocolate Sauce · Opposite - Lemon Tart with Berries and Spun Sugar

While remaining faithful to the sound foundations of the classics, Chef/Owner Larry Rogers successfully combines his love for the simplicity of Italian food with the varied tastes of his Caribbean heritage. The delicious end result of Larry's novel approach is a refreshingly different style of cuisine that reflects a level of honest integrity that veers away from the 'fuss and fancy' that nowadays tends to dominate many of the more elegant establishments of the world.

The heart and soul of Larry's food is his ability to blend a variety of flavours and textures that produce sublimely simple dishes; such as the "Jerk Pork Gnocchi", which integrates the spiciness of the Caribbean with the soft sweetness of peas, coupled with gnocchi of the Mediterranean. Larry's emphasis is on using fresh seasonal ingredients, holding fast onto the unbreachable rule tantamount to all great chefs that there must be "no compromise on quality". This approach to his cuisine gives Larry a loyal following both local and foreign.

Larry's culinary walk began 20 years ago in New Zealand where he got a sound footing in the classics, working with "imported" European chefs. After leaving New Zealand he then travelled and worked his way through Europe and the United States, finally making his way back home to the shores of Barbados.

Potato Gnocchi with "Jerk Pork" on a Sweet Pea Puree
Serves four

Ingredients
200g pork tenderloin (trimmed)
Jerk seasoning
Oil for searing

1kg potatoes
(Russet or Idaho preferably)
150g flour
3 egg yolks
Salt and pepper
Fresh nutmeg
Parmesan cheese
Chives

1 medium onion (finely diced)
1 medium leek (finely diced)
500g green peas
300ml cream
100g butter

Method:
For the pork:
Rub the pork with the jerk seasoning and rest in the fridge for about 2 hours (the longer you leave it the bigger the flavour).

For the pea puree:
In a pot, sweat the onions and leeks in butter (on a low heat) without colour until tender. Add the peas and cream, bring to the boil and simmer for 5 minutes. Season with a little salt and pepper, then puree the mixture. At this stage the puree can be passed through a sieve for a smooth refined puree or left as is for a somewhat coarser texture. Check your seasoning.

For the gnocchi:
Bake the potatoes in a 350 degree Fahrenheit pre-heated oven for 1 hour or until they are completely cooked. Split the potatoes and scoop out the flesh and puree through a potato ricer. Place the hot potato on countertop and make a well in the centre. Place a layer of about half a cup of flour in the well, add egg yolks then another half cup more of flour with salt, pepper and grated nutmeg. This process should be done quickly (no more the 60 seconds) as overworking the dough will make the gnocchi heavy and sticky. Add a little more flour if necessary. Shape into a ball and roll in flour. Pull off a section of dough and roll it by hand on a lightly floured surface into a "snake ", about half an inch thick. Cut into half inch pieces and using two fingers lightly squeeze the centre of each piece. Test one gnocchi by placing it in a large pot of rapidly boiling salted water. It is cooked as soon as it floats to the surface. To remove gnocchi from the pot with ease, use a slotted spoon. Try gnocchi for seasoning and add more flour if the gnocchi seems too mushy. Continue forming the gnocchi, placing them on a floured tray. Then cook in the boiling water. Place cooked gnocchi into a bowl of iced water for approx. 2 minutes then remove and drain on a paper towel. In a 12 inch pan, heat olive oil at medium heat, sauté gnocchi for 2-3mins or until lightly golden.

To serve:
In a small pan, heat oil on a high heat and sear off the seasoned pork on all sides. Place in a hot oven (400 degrees Fahrenheit) for 10 minutes or until the pork is cooked inside to 160 degrees temperature (or pinkish in colour). Remove and rest to the side. Meanwhile, in a 12 inch pan heat oil to a medium to high heat and add gnocchi; cook by tossing gently for 2 to 3 minutes until lightly golden colour. Reheat the pea puree and place in a serving dish. Arrange gnocchi in the center, then add thin slices of the "jerk pork" around the gnocchi. Sprinkle the gnocchi with grated parmesan and chives to garnish if desired.

lone star

This elegant and stylishly appointed restaurant benefits from both an outstanding location and a vibrant atmosphere, with an open plan kitchen adding even more to the sense of theatre

From the time that it was first opened in December 1997, Lone Star quickly established itself as one of the elite restaurants on the island. The Lone Star concept, which was created and designed by co-owner Steve Cox, is in essence contemporary and minimalist. Set right on a superb beach in St. James, with spectacular views out over the Caribbean Sea, this elegant and stylishly appointed restaurant benefits from both an outstanding location and a vibrant atmosphere, with an open plan kitchen adding even more to the sense of theatre. In keeping with this theme, Lone Star is considered by many to be the 'see and be seen' spot on the west coast.

General Manager Rory Rodger and his team always strive for perfection and, as a result of their efforts, Lone Star was named as one of the top 50 restaurants in the world by Restaurant Magazine in February 2002.

Above - Tuna Tartare with Fresh Papaya Salad · Opposite - Thai Green Curry Shrimp with Jasmine Rice

Opposite - Blackened Dolphin with Sweet Potato Mash & Papaya Lime Salsa

Above left - Marinated Crispy "Jerk" Pork with Jasmine Rice & Pimento Pepper Sauce

Above right - Medley of Seafood with Shrimp, Scallops & Calamari in Puff Pastry with Fine Herbs

Above - Apple Tarte Tartin with Caramel Cream Sauce & Toffee Wafer
Opposite - Warmed Chocolate Brownie with Vanilla Ice Cream & White Chocolate Sauce

The menu at Lone Star is filled with eclectic selections of seafood and caviar, Indian Baltis, Chinese , Thai dishes and Mediterranean cuisine. The chef at Lone Star comes from the company's two London restaurants, Prego and The Wharf. For the current season, Mr. Michael Bull is the overall manager of the kitchen. He initially came over to The Lone Star in 2000 as the oriental chef, having previously trained with David Kan in London, to pass on his skills and train the local Barbadian chefs in this fine culinary art. The company also takes Barbadian staff over to the two London restaurants in the off-season for further training and an opportunity for them to gain valuable international experience.

Thai Green Curry Shrimp

Step 1 – Curry Paste
Grind the following ingredients in a pestle & mortar:

10g cloves
10g black pepper
10g coriander seeds
10g cumin seeds
10g white pepper

Blitz the following ingredients together in a food processor:

1 bulb garlic
1 inch stem ginger
2 banana shallots
2 bunches fresh coriander
3 sticks lemon grass
4 large red chilies
20g turmeric

Mix the above steps together, along with following ingredients, into a smooth paste:

1 cup Num Pla fish sauce
1/2 cup vegetable oil
1/2 cup lime juice

Step 2 – Thai Green Curry Sauce (serves 4-6 portions)
1 medium white onion
1/4 bunch coriander
2 cloves garlic
1/4 inch stem ginger
1 liter coconut milk
75ml sweet coconut cream
1oz Tom Yum paste
6 stems lemon grass
2 shots Num Pla fish sauce
1 large dessert spoon Green Curry Paste

1. Finely chop the onion, coriander, garlic and ginger. Cook lightly, without colour, over a medium flame.
2. Add Tom Yum paste and Green Curry Paste to pan and mix in. Stir for 4 minutes.
3. Add all remaining ingredients, leaving lemon grass whole, and slowly reduce by a third.

Step 3
Main – Per Portion
6-8 shelled and de-veined shrimp
1/2 medium sliced white onion
4 florets of broccoli
3 okras halved
4-6 fine green beans

In a thick bottom pan, put a little sesame & vegetable oil (1/2 & 1/2) add 1/2 a small finely chopped onion, cook without colour for one minute, add shrimps then after another minute add in the Broccoli, Okra and Beans. Add the sauce and cook out until the shrimps are cooked.

N.B. Be careful not to over cook the shrimp!

Step 4 – To Serve
Hot Jasmine infused rice
Sweet basil leaves
Optional: Side dish of Poppadoms, Raita and Tamarind & Mango Chutney

mullins

Whether it be for lunch or dinner, Mullins is a very picturesque location to enjoy good food and friendly social imbibement.

Ideally situated on one of the finest beaches in Barbados, Mullins now ranks as one of the most fashionable Beach Restaurants on the West Coast. The Barbadian Head Chef Michael Harrison and Manager Nicholas Gittens both bring with them a wealth of restaurant experience and together they run Mullins with a refreshing sense of Caribbean flair. Whether it be for lunch or dinner, Mullins is a very picturesque location to enjoy good food and friendly social imbibement. Lunch features an exciting array of light and tasty beachside favourites, with a menu that caters to both adults and children. Dinner, on the other hand, offers a more sophisticated menu, but without sacrificing any of its typically relaxed Bajan warmth and charm.   A wide selection of drinks and cocktails can be enjoyed any time of the day or night on one of the two well positioned terraces. Mullins is well known for being one of the most spectacular settings on the island to watch the sun set of an evening.

Above - Tomato & Zucchini Tart with Arugula, Shaved Parmesan & Pesto · Opposite - Open Faced Flying Fish Sandwich with Curry Slaw

Opposite - Tower of Grilled Chicken, Lobster, Potatoes, Mango and Avocado Salsa
Above left - Grilled Caribbean Shrimps, Olive Potatoes, Tomato Fondue with Alfalfa Sprouts
Above right - Olive Crusted Dolphin, Sautéed Vegetables, Pink Peppercorn & Ginger Sauce

Opposite - Banana Tart Tatin with Aged Spiced Rum Ice Cream & Caramelised Bajan Cherries

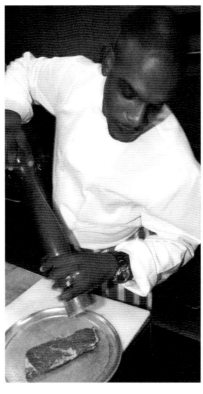

Awarded a bronze medal in the 'Taste of the Caribbean Culinary Competition' in 1999 and named Barbados' 'Chef of the Year' at the 2001 Minister of Tourism Awards, Head Chef Michael Harrison is committed to "preparing excellent, imaginative food, using only top quality ingredients". In addition to working at several top hotels and restaurants in Barbados prior to taking up his position at Mullins, Michael has also benefited from several stints at a number of high quality overseas establishments such as Gleneagles in Scotland; the White Barn Inn in Maine, USA; and, notably, he worked at Le Gavroche in London for a period of 18 months under the direction of the renowned Chef Michel Roux Jr.

Tower of Grilled Coriander & Ginger Chicken, Breadfruit and Lobster Brandade, Mango/Avocado Salsa with Mango Essence

Ingredients

4 Chicken Breasts

Ingredients - Marinade for Chicken:

4ozs Tomato Ketchup

1oz Ginger Peel & Grate

Juice and zest of 1 orange

1 tbsp soy sauce

2 bunches chopped coriander

2 tbsps sugar

4 tbsps sesame oil

4 tbsps olive oil

2 cloves of diced garlic

Ingredients - Mango and Avocado Salsa

a ripe mango

an avocado

1 small onion

Juice of 1 lime

Coriander leaves

1 small tomato peel and dice

Ingredients - Mango Essence

2 mangoes peel and puree

3ozs coconut milk

1 small onion

2 cloves of garlic

2 star anise

4 cardamoms

Ginger

1 tsp red curry paste

2 tsps passion puree

Ingredients - Breadfruit and Lobster Brandade

1 small breadfruit, cook and puree

1 small lobster, cook and dice

1 small onion, dice with parsley, dill and thyme

2 tbsp garlic butter

Grilled vegetables, okras, bell peppers, eggplant, tomato and finger squash, all diced

Method - Marinade for Chicken:

Whisk all ingredients together and place chicken in the mixture to marinate for 24 hours.

Method - Mango and Avocado Salsa

Dice the avocado and mango, place in a bowl and add all other ingredients, season to taste with salt and pepper.

Method - Mango Essence

In a hot pan with a little butter, add the onion, garlic, ginger, star anise, sauté for a few minutes, add all other ingredients. Cook for 30 minutes on a low heat.

Method - Breadfruit and Lobster Brandade

Heat a pan, add the butter and onion mixture sweat for a few minutes, add all other ingredients, and combine well.

Parmesan Cheese Basket and Disc

3ozs grated parmesan

Using a small ring on a non-stick tray, place some cheese in the ring and repeat it seven more times. In a hot oven, place tray and allow the cheese to melt. Using two cups shape four of the cheese discs into the basket and leave the other four flat.

Garnish

Chicken livers sautéed in red wine

Herb oil, fried glass noodles and basil

To Assemble

On a plate, place ring in the centre, fill with breadfruit brandade lift the ring off, put the parmesan disc and the cooked chicken on the breadfruit, top with the basket of chicken livers, salsa and garnish. Finish with mango essence and herb oil.

olives

Olive's is located in an old coral stone building with both air-conditioned and outside eating areas. There is also an upstairs cocktail bar where light meals may be enjoyed in a warm and friendly atmosphere.

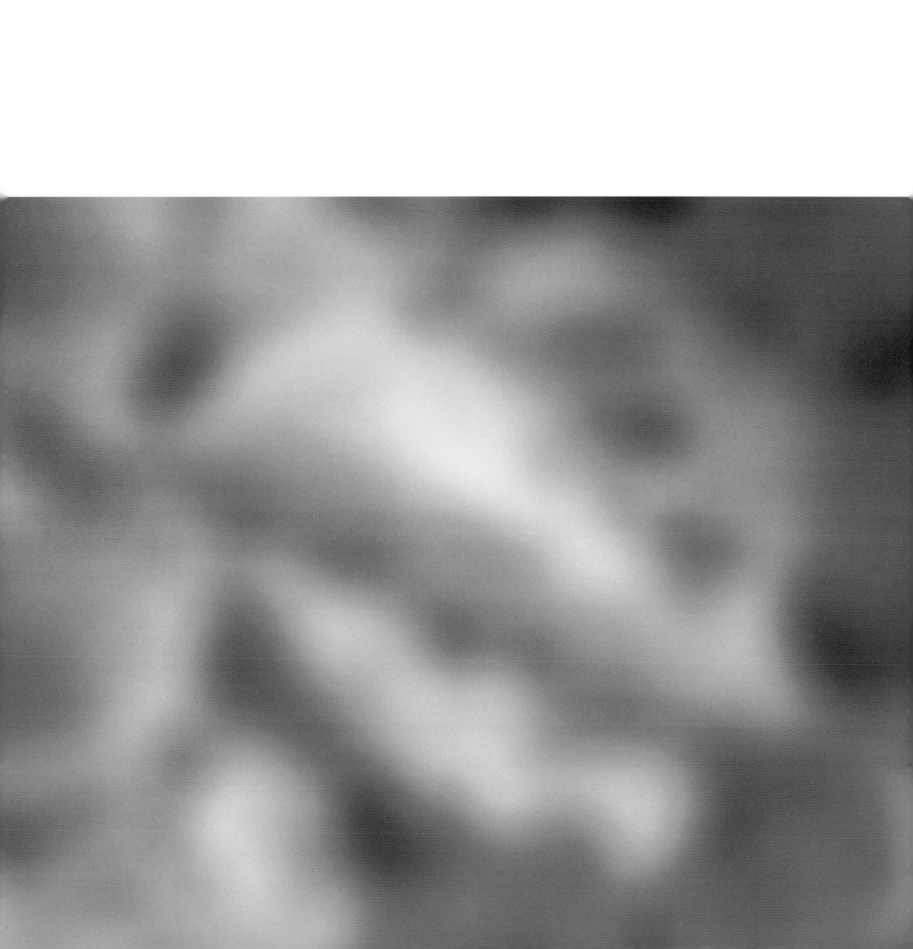

Olive's, in Holetown on the island's west coast, is located in an old coral stone building with both air-conditioned and outside eating areas. There is also an upstairs cocktail bar where light meals may be enjoyed in a warm and friendly atmosphere.

The food at Olive's is essentially Mediterranean with a little Bajan twist; an appealing fusion which is achieved by trying to use as many local ingredients as possible but also incorporating high quality products imported from Europe to complement the style of Olive's bistro oriented cuisine. The food is very much simple 'comfort food' with cleverly fused flavours supported by an outstanding wine.

Above - Nage of Seafood · Opposite - Deep Fried Thai Breaded Shrimp with a Mint and Coriander Dressing and Asparagus

Opposite - Pan Fried Grouper sat on Bok-Choy with a Rich Red Wine Sauce

Above - Seared Lobster and Scallops with a Tapenade Dressing on a Rosemary Skewer

Above - Fillet of Black Belly Sheep served with a trio of Offal (Heart, Kidney and Liver), sat on Anna Potato, Cabbage and a Red Wine Sauce

Opposite - Baked Lobster topped with Crab Meat and Ratatouille and a Herb-Crust

Chocolate Fondant served with a Mango Sorbet

The chef, Scott Ames, is from England, where he trained in a number of Michelin star restaurants, learning both classical French and modern English cuisine. Growing up in the area of the New Forest, Scott developed a love for going out into the woods and picking anything from wild mushrooms to Fraise de Bois to Crab Apples. Here in Barbados, Scott's love for using the best and freshest local produce focuses on the ready availability of a wide variety of fresh fish of exceptional quality. The Olive's 'Specials' reflect that passion in the way that they consist purely of freshly caught fish, and not just the usual selection that generally pop up on menus throughout the island. Scott prepares and serves his fish dishes in any number of different styles, all of which will give any fish lover a delight.

Deep Fried Thai Breaded Shrimp
Serves 4

Ingredients

12 large shrimp with end of tail remaining, 'butterflied' down the back
Small amount of Red Thai Curry Paste
1 Egg
Breadcrumbs
Coriander
1 tub of Yogurt
Lime Juice
Cayenne Pepper
Fresh Mint

Method

Take a small amount of the red Thai Curry Paste and the egg and mix them in a bowl. Take the coriander and finely chop and mix it into the breadcrumbs. Dip the shrimp into the paste and then into the bread crumbs. You will need to deep fry these for about two minutes and let them rest for another two minutes before serving. If you overcook them they will become tough and will shrink.

For the sauce, place the yogurt into a liquidizer with a small bunch of mint and coriander. People's taste will vary on the strength of the herbs, so it's better to start off with less of the herbs and add more later if required. Blend this to a puree and then add the Cayenne Pepper, lime juice and a little salt and pepper to taste.

pisces

Perhaps no other restaurant in Barbados better reflects the Caribbean and its wonderful array of top quality seafood than Pisces.

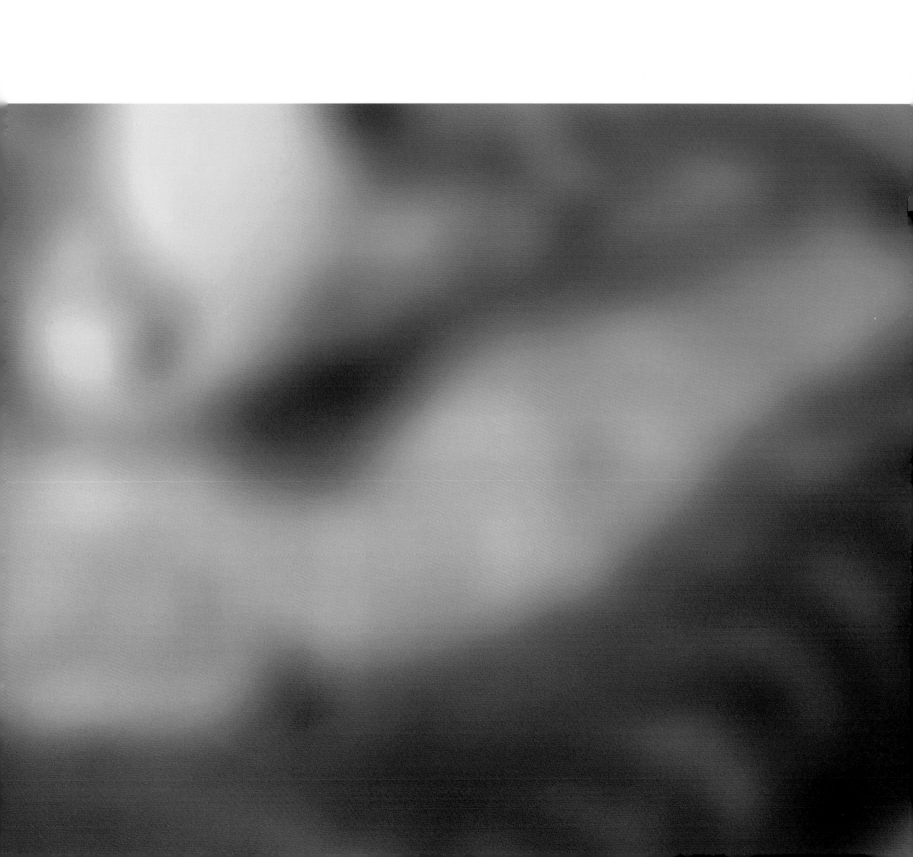

Above - Conch and Squid Salad with Glass Noodles and Coriander Vinaigrette

Perhaps no other restaurant in Barbados better reflects the Caribbean and its wonderful array of top quality seafood than Pisces. Located on the scenic coastal corner of St. Lawrence Gap, this trendy oceanside restaurant with its lush tropical ambience puts to rest the saying "the more spectacular the view, the less spectacular the food."

Pisces was first established in 1972 by Dr. William Donawa who claims to have opened the restaurant simply so he could have "a good place to eat." Over the course of the years since then, Pisces has earned its place among the finest restaurants, successfully combining good food, a unique ambience and excellent service.

Previous page left - Baby Octopus Salad · Previous page right - Tempura Prawns with Roasted Peanut Relish and red wine reduction.
Above - Pisces Sampler Plate – Grilled Yellow Fin Tuna, Blackened Mahi Mahi, Rock Crab Claw, Mussels and two sauces
Opposite - Lobster and Sour Mango Salad with Heart of Palm and a Balsamic Emulsion.

Opposite - Caramelised Banana Galette – Peanut Brittle, Vanilla Bean Ice Cream and Banana Chip.
Above - Coconut Milk Ice Cream with a Toasted Coconut Cookie.

Under the leadership of the current Executive Chef/Owner, David Farouk, 'vision, attention to detail and style' are the modern hallmarks of Pisces. Along with David Farouk, two Barbadians, Chef Anderson Hunt and Executive Sous Chef Jason Gittens, head up the kitchen team, whose style of incorporating local seafood and herbs into a classically based cuisine results in elegant and intensely flavourful food.

David Farouk, who also has Caribbean roots, started his career in the culinary world at the tender age of 16. He attended the culinary Arts Programme at Malaspina University College in British Columbia. He later did his apprenticeship in the classical French style under Master Chef Pierre Koffel at Deep Cove Chalet, British Columbia. His graduate studies were completed at the Culinary Institute of America in High Park, New York. After spending a few years working in fine restaurants in Hong Kong, Toronto, Australia and San Francisco, he returned to the Caribbean in 1996 taking on the role of Executive Chef at Pisces.

Chef David Farouk says: "I have been greatly influenced by Alan Ducasse, a very contemporary and avant-garde chef whose cuisine has always been elegantly fashionable but who has never strayed away from food combinations, flavours and textures that work well together. My personal philosophy on food involves the use of the freshest ingredients while applying international techniques. Working at Pisces, where the focus is on Caribbean seafood, is especially exciting. I feel that I have a unique opportunity to develop a truly Caribbean Cuisine."

Baby Octopus Salad
Serves 6

Ingredients:

1lb. Baby Octopus
1/2 green sweet pepper
1/2 red sweet pepper
30g finely diced red onions
1tbsp minced bonnet peppers
2tbsp finely chopped flat leafed parsley
2tbsp finely chopped cilantro
2fl oz extra virgin olive oil
2fl oz white vinegar
Salt and black pepper to taste
Fresh cilantro sprigs
4tbsp sesame oil

Method:

Make sure to thoroughly clean and de-beak the octopus. Place the octopus in a steamer, and steam for 7 to 10 minutes. Remove octopus from steamer and refresh in an ice bath. Finely slice the body and upper tentacles of the octopus and combine with diced sweet pepper, red onions and cilantro. In a separate bowl, mix all the other ingredients and adjust seasoning to suit.

Before serving, thoroughly combine the two mixtures and let stand for 30 minutes. Serve in 4-oz portions, using fresh cilantro sprigs and sesame oil to garnish.

sakura

As is the case in most sushi restaurants in the world, many of Sakura's patrons enjoy sitting at the sushi bar where they can have a close-up view of the chef, Taigo, as he performs his magical food art, and then ask to sample whatever takes their fancy at the time.

Sakura is the only sushi restaurant in Barbados. Located in Holetown, Sakura first opened its doors in 1999 and it has been very popular with Barbadians and visitors alike ever since. As is the case in most sushi restaurants in the world, many of Sakura's patrons enjoy sitting at the sushi bar where they can have a close-up view of the chef, Taigo, as he performs his magical food art, and then ask to sample whatever takes their fancy at the time.

Opposite - Sashimi • Above - Ika (Baby Squid)

Above - Deluxe Bento Box · Opposite - The Dragon
Following page left - Nigiri · Following page right - Ama Ebi (Sweet Shrimp)

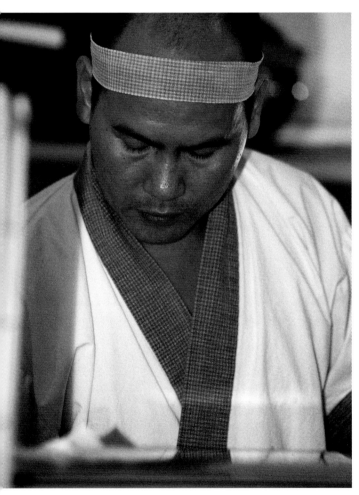

Taigo is both the manager and the chef at Sakura, and he brings with him over 18 years of experience in the restaurant business and a special flair for creating a wide variety of Asian food. Part way during his career Taigo decided to focus on sushi and so trained to become a sushi chef. Prior to opening Sakura, he worked at Masa Matsuri in Toronto, Canada for four years. Taigo's current 'Bay Area Sushi' style is influenced by the experiences he gained with Hokkaido and Fuji in San Francisco, where he worked for a period of seven years.

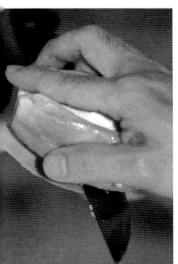

"Tokyo-Style" Vinegar Pickled Ginger Slices

Ingredients
1/2 sheet nori
2 slices cuttlefish (Ika)
1 cucumber
4 slices tuna fish (Maguro)
4 yellow tail (Hamachi)
4 salmon (Sake)
3 slices Seabream (Izumidai)
1 shrimp
3 slices mackerel (Saba)
2 slices Japanese Egg Roll
4 slices of pickled radish (Taikuan)
Wasabi ginger

Method
Place the sushi rice (recipe below) in a serving dish. Cut the nori into fine shreds and sprinkle it on top. Arrange the tuna, yellow tail, salmon and other ingredients neatly on the sushi rice.

Cut the cucumber into thin diagonal slices. Place the pickled radish on the side as a garnish, then top with wasabi ginger and serve.

Sushi Rice (Serves 4)
Wash 2 cups of rice (short grain or sushi rice), draining it until the rice is clean, white and translucent. Add 1 1/2 cups of water and soak for 30 minutes. Cook the rice in an electric rice cooker (or on an electric or gas stove) until done. Pour the sushi vinegar (recipe below) over the cooked rice while the rice is still hot, and mix it in with a rice paddle. Continue mixing until the rice is light and fluffy and the flavor of the vinegar is dispersed.

Sushi Vinegar
Add a teaspoon of salt to 3 tablespoons of rice vinegar and bring to a boil over low heat. Add 2 tablespoons of granulated white sugar and turn off the heat immediately. The vinegar mixture is ready when the sugar has completely dissolved. The proportion of sugar to vinegar can be adjusted according to personal taste.

the cliff

The Cliff, located right on the edge of the sea, has a wonderful location and it has been cleverly designed to maximize the magical ambience of its surroundings. Yet, when first time diners recall their experience at The Cliff, it is usually the excellent quality of the food that they praise most.

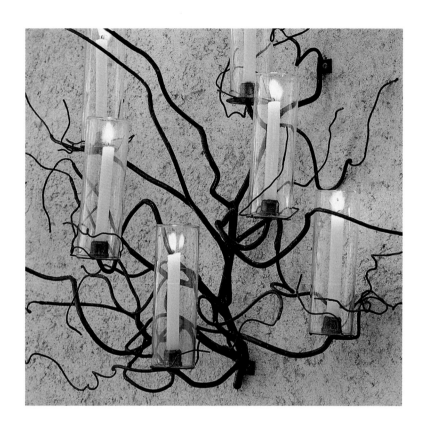

First opened in 1995 and now firmly established as one of the very top and most popular restaurants in Barbados, The Cliff always has a dedicated following of repeat clientele, both locals and visitors alike, including a long list of international celebrities. The Cliff, located right on the edge of the sea, has a wonderful location and it has been cleverly designed to maximize the magical ambience of its surroundings. Yet, when first time diners recall their experience at The Cliff, it is usually the excellent quality of the food that they praise most.

Opposite - Pan Seared Red Snapper on Creamed Potatoes with Sweet Pea Reduction and Tartare Sauce

Above - Cajun Salmon on a Spicy Eggplant Salsa with Indian Curry Oil and Minted Cucumber Relish

Above - Fillet of Beef Tenderloin, Grilled Portobello Mushroom, Tarragon Jus, Roasted Pearl Onions
Opposite - Seared Tuna with Sweet Potato Cake, Curried Sweetcorn Sauce and Tomato Salsa

Opposite - An assortment of Sushi with Tuna Tartare, Tobiko, Wasabi, Ginger & Soy

Above - Strawberry Tart with Creme Bruleé Custard and Strawberry Coulis

Above · Iced Coffee · Cognac Parfait with Wafers · Opposite · Chocolate Dome filled with Chocolate Hazelnut Mousse with Vanilla Cream

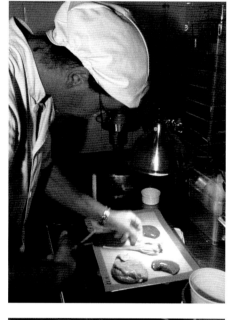

Head Chef Paul Owens, who was born in Liverpool, England, consistently creates an eclectic variety of exquisite dishes. Paul, who has a special flair for combining contrasting flavours and textures to produce deliciously interesting cuisine, gives extra variety to his menu by producing a selection of "specials" each night. He also uses his own relatively simple style of presentation to ensure that every single dish that comes out of his kitchen looks 'ready to photograph', even though he himself insists that this is "no big deal" and that it is the way the food tastes that really matters.

Paul first trained in England, where he gained valuable experience working in a number of busy and successful kitchens before moving to Barbados. He initially made a name for himself at Treasure Beach Hotel, which was owned and operated at that time by the Ward family. He then moved on to Carambola with Brian Ward for several successful years, before this 'dynamic duo' then teamed up again to open The Cliff. Brian Ward, who owns the property, was the man who had the vision to conceive the master plan for this dramatic restaurant.

Paul Owens has a deceptively simple approach to his cooking: "There is no need to try and be elaborate. A good piece of steak or fish can only be made into a good meal if it is prepared properly and then served with a good sauce and good garnish. It's all about quality, everything on the plate must be good. Just keep it simple, but make it the best!"

Paul is always the first to acknowledge the support he is given by his dedicated team at The Cliff, emphasizing that he "couldn't do it without them". His final word: "Being at The Cliff has given me the chance to meet and make friends with so many interesting people from all around the world who I would never have met otherwise".

Cajun Style Salmon on a Spicy Eggplant Salsa with Indian Curry Oil, Coriander Vinaigrette and Minted Cucumber Relish

Ingredients:

The Salmon
4 x 5oz salmon fillets
Cajun seasoning mixed with a little flour
for coating salmon
4oz clarified butter

Minted Cucumber Relish
1 cucumber (seeded and diced)
1 cup natural yogurt
1 small red onion (diced)
Bunch of chopped fresh mint (or 1 tbsp
mint sauce)
1 tbsp mayonnaise (optional)

The Curry Oil
2 tbsps hot Indian curry paste
3 tbsps sherry wine vinegar
8-10 fl.oz grapeseed oil or olive oil
Salt & Pepper (to taste)

Coriander Vinaigrette
2 tbsps red wine vinegar
1/2 cup olive oil
2 cups coriander
1 tbsp lime juice
1 tbsp garlic (chopped)
2 tbsp red onions (chopped)
2 tbsp honey
Salt & Pepper

Spicy Eggplant Salsa
1 large eggplant (diced)
A little olive oil
4 small red onions (diced)
1/2 tsp ground cumin
1/2 tsp cardamom (ground)
4 tbsp diced sweet gerkins
1 tbsp garam masala
Small bunch of basil leaves (chopped)
Small bunch of coriander leaves (chopped)
Small bunch of chives (chopped)
Salt & Pepper
2 tsp sherry vinegar

Method:
Mix all the ingredients for the MInted Cucumber Relish and put aside.

For the Curry Oil, using a whisk, mix the curry paste with the vinegar and slowly add the oil. Season to taste, and put into a squeezy bottle. Can be kept for weeks in a refrigerator.

Blend all ingredients for the Coriander Vinaigrette together except the oil. Add the oil slowly until emulsified and season with salt and pepper. Place in a squeezy bottle and refrigerate.

For the Spicy Eggplant Salsa sauté the eggplant in the olive oil with the onion over medium heat until soft. Add the vinegar, spices and gerkins. Place into a bowl and add the herbs. Season to taste and refrigerate until needed.

To Assemble:
Heat the clarified butter in a large non-stick pan. Coat the salmon with the cajun seasoning and cook about 3 minutes each side. You want the salmon to be pink inside. Place the eggplant salsa in the centre of 4 bowls and warm in the oven. Place the salmon on the salsa; squeeze some curry oil around the salmon with the coriander vinaigrette. Using a teaspoon carefully place some cucumber relish around the plate and garnish with coriander leaves.

the country club

The beautifully designed Country Club Restaurant is spacious and open, offering a very conducive environment for elegantly casual dining. The varied menu and wine list successfully live up to the high standards generally expected of Sandy Lane Hotel and the service is first class.

The location of the Country Club at Sandy Lane, which sits high on a ridge above the west coast, provides the welcome combination of a spectacular view across the golf course to the sea, accompanied by a refreshingly cool breeze. The beautifully designed Country Club Restaurant is spacious and open, offering a very conducive environment for elegantly casual dining. The varied menu and wine list successfully live up to the high standards generally expected of Sandy Lane Hotel and the service is first class.

Opposite - BBQ Teriayki Shrimp, Homemade Spring Rolls, Tempura Vegetables, Samosas and Buttermilk Onion Rings
Above - House Salad with Roasted Plum Dressing

Above - Seared Fillet of Red Snapper, Fragrant Basmati Rice, Wilted Greens and Chilli-Coriander Oil
Opposite - Roasted Fillet of Black Angus Beef, Caramelised Onions, Pecan Mash and Red Wine Jus

Opposite - Traditional Panna Cotta served with Spiced Cold Soup and Assorted Fresh Fruits

Above - Lime & Vanilla Creme Bruleé - Caramelised, served with a Citrus Sour Cream Ice Cream & Fresh Fruits

All of the restaurants at Sandy Lane are overseen by the Australian Executive Chef, Mark Patten. By the age of twenty-two he was already Executive Chef of Quarter Sessions, an award-winning restaurant in Melbourne. His career then took him all over the world, so that by the time he moved to Barbados in 1999 to join the Sandy Lane team, Mark had worked and trained in a variety of top class restaurants in places as diverse as Malaysia, Norway, Cyprus and London. The new Sandy Lane was Mark's third experience of opening a five star property.

With the understanding of the highest level of quality and attention to detail, Sandy Lane's restaurants and bars are the "Theatre" for the hotel. The food needs to be powerful and diverse, using only the finest local and imported products to enhance the skills of the culinary team, a rule that Mark Patten has adopted throughout his whole career in the kitchen.

The Sous Chef at the Country Club Restaurant is Barbadian Timothy Ricardo Walker. Prior to joining Sandy Lane some seven years ago, Timothy had worked in a wide variety of restaurants in Barbados and elsewhere in the Caribbean, as well as serving as Executive Chef for the United States Ambassador to Barbados. Since being at Sandy Lane, Timothy has had the honour of preparing meals for famous world leaders such as Bill Clinton and Fidel Castro.

Tamarind Glazed Fillet of Beef served with Walnut Sweet Potato Mash, Maderia and Shallot Sauce

Ingredients

1-8 oz Fillet of Beef

2 oz Tamarind Puree

16 oz beef stock

1/2 bottle of Maderia

1 kg potatoes

3 oz milk

2 oz butter

1 oz crushed walnuts

1 oz diced shallots

Method:

Beef:

Rub the beef with virgin olive oil, salt and cracked black pepper. Place the beef on a hot clean grill until cooked as required, then remove.

Sauce:

Sautee the shallots gently in a saucepan with some fresh butter; then add the maderia wine to the shallots. When the wine is reduced add the beef stock; reduce some more and season with salt and pepper. For additional taste you can also whisk in some butter. This is optional.

Walnut Mash:

Boil potatoes in a pot until soft, then remove and drain. In another saucepan, warm the milk and butter together, remove from heat and add this mixture to the potato. Whisk together until soft and creamy, then add salt, pepper and walnuts.

Setting up the dish:

Using the plate of your choice, place a four inch ring in the centre of the plate, and pack the mash potato inside. Remove the ring, place the beef on top of the mash, drizzle some of the tamarind sauce over the beef, then add the maderia sauce around the mash on the plate. Garnish with some fried julienne of leek and eggplant on top of the beef.

the fish pot

Possibly one of the island's most picturesque locations, The Fish Pot at Little Good Harbour, is situated on a particularly attractive stretch of the St.Peter coastline.

Possibly one of the island's most picturesque locations, The Fish Pot at Little Good Harbour, situated on a particularly attractive stretch of the St.Peter coastline, has become one of Barbados' most fashionable restaurants. Housed in part of a converted fort and boasting an unpretentious, casual style of restaurant with ample panache, this little spot has all the appeal of what a Caribbean island restaurant should be. Set between two fish markets just North of Six Mens Bay, where traditional, master craftsmen can still be seen building and repairing their fishing boats, this area is quite often described as "what Barbados was like 20 years ago".

Opposite - Seared Herb-Crusted Tuna on a Nicoise Salad

Above - Stuffed Calamari with a Pesto Parfait and Roasted Pepper Coulis

Above - Seared Scallops with a Tomato and Rocket Salad on Basil and Garlic Aioli

Opposite - Grilled Kingfish with Steamed Mussels and Arugula Cream

Opposite - Duo of Crème Brulèe Vanilla and Nutmeg with Fruit Basket · Above - Walnut Cheesecake with Pistachio Ice Cream

The Barbadian Executive Chef at The Fish Pot, Stephen Belgrave, has created a menu inspired by the sea, using only the freshest of produce available to him, and infusing it with local herbs, spices and fruit, creating a fresh and exciting array of dishes to choose from. With the fish market just a stone's throw away from the restaurant, it is inevitable that delicious seafood dishes will feature prominently on the menu.

Stephen's interest in cooking started at a young age because his father was very handy in the kitchen and he taught his children how to cook. His first job in the field of cuisine was at Josef's Restaurant where he served as an apprentice chef and was trained in international cuisine for three years.

While working at Josef's, Stephen enrolled at The Barbados Culinary School. Upon graduation he worked at several local restaurants and hotels, and also travelled to England where he trained at such fine establishments as the Chester Grosvenor, The Stafford Hotel, The Connaught, Le Gavroche and Quaglino's. On returning to Barbados he spent one year at Coral Reef and then moved to his current position as Head Chef at The Fish Pot.

Stephen describes his style of cooking: "With my experience in Barbados and overseas, I use a fusion of local and international foods to create dishes which have international flair but still retain the flavours of the Caribbean. I believe that to create flavourful dishes you must love and appreciate food and have the patience to present it in an appealing manner".

Shrimp in a Thai Bouillabaise

Ingredients:

8 large shrimp
1 red bell pepper
1 onion
1 sprig of thyme and marjoram
2 cloves of garlic
1/2 tsp of red Thai curry paste
1/2 tsp of tomato paste
1/2 tsp of shrimp paste
2 cups of fish stock
1/2 cup of coconut milk
1/2 cup of heavy cream
1 tbsp of olive oil
4 cherry tomatoes cut in half
4 small mushrooms cut in half

Method:

Finely chop the red pepper, onion, garlic, thyme and marjoram. Take 3 of the large shrimp and cut them into pieces. Heat the frying pan and add olive oil. Sauté the chopped ingredients with the shrimp. Add red Thai curry, tomato and shrimp paste. Cook lightly for 2-3 minutes. Add the fish stock and reduce to half. Then add the cream and coconut milk. Reduce until the consistency has thickened slightly and blend.
Season the remaining shrimp with lime juice, salt, and pepper. Sauté the shrimp with cherry tomatoes and mushrooms. Add the sauce to the shrimp and simmer for 1-2 minutes. Serve with basmati rice.

the sandpiper

The Sandpiper is a charming open-air restaurant, nestled in a luxuriant garden setting, surrounded by waterfalls and fish ponds. Along with the restaurant's attractive Barbadian architecture, the beauty of the natural surroundings combine to create a welcome atmosphere of relaxation and peace.

Opened in 1971 and located in the hotel of the same name, The Sandpiper Restaurant has long been considered one of the best on the island in recognition of its overall consistency; its high standard of service and cuisine; and its extensive and well rounded wine list. The many repeat clients of The Sandpiper rate the food and service at the restaurant as their main reasons for returning again and again.

Owned and managed by the O'Hara and Capaldi families, who also own and operate The Coral Reef Club, The Sandpiper is a charming open-air restaurant nestled in a luxuriant garden setting, surrounded by waterfalls and fish ponds. Along with the restaurant's attractive Barbadian architecture, the beauty of the natural surroundings combine to create a welcome atmosphere of relaxation and peace.

The charming Bar Lounge at The Sandpiper is a perfect rendezvous for pre or post dinner drinks and serves a truly tempting selection of classic cocktails and aperitifs. The restaurant features light entertainment, solos, duos or trios, every night in the winter season or every other night in the summer season.

Above - Mako Shark Ceviche with Sesame Flat Bread • Opposite - Tuna Tartare

Above - Salt Crusted Grouper with Soused Cucumber & Creole Tomato Jam · Opposite - Sandpiper's Hot Pot of the Sea

Opposite - Bajan Cherry & Pineapple Sorbet Parfait with Toasted Marshmallow
Above - White Chocolate Banana & Macadamia Nut Pudding with Dark Chocolate & Cointreau

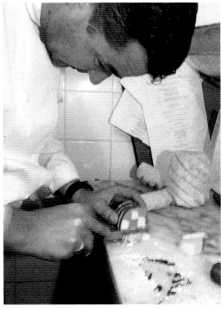

The talented team of Barbadian chefs at Sandpiper, under the direction of Executive Chef Scott Williams, always aims to create 'excitement on the plate and on the palate' with their unique culinary style. The Sandpiper chefs have found success in combining ingredients and methods from far and wide that on first inspection might appear curious, but in the final taste test prove to be deliciously rewarding. Scott Williams honed his skills at a number of highly regarded restaurants in his home country of England, including the Michelin rated Hambleton Hall and Capitol Hotel. His talents earned him a spot as junior sous chef at Quaglinos, the Conran designed eatery which prepares gourmet fare for up to one thousand persons per day. From there he went to work for Richard Branson, of Virgin fame, as Executive Chef on Necker Island. This stint on Branson's private island allowed Scott to fine tune his personal style of cooking for a smaller, though just as discerning clientele. Scott enjoys having access to the best of local and imported ingredients as he and his talented team impress Sandpiper diners with inventive daily changing menus. He is especially thrilled with the excellent fresh fish that is available in Barbados.

Scott refers to his style as 'modern eclectic'. His philosophy is that: "We go out to dine in order to experience something extraordinary; and so I aim to provide that with every dish."

Sandpiper's Hot Pot of the Sea

Ingredients

For the Broth:

1 cup dry white wine

2 cups vermouth (Noilly Prat)

1 cup good fish stock

2 shallots finely chopped

1 large onion finely chopped

1 clove garlic finely chopped

1 tsp. thyme leaves

1/2 tsp. crushed fennel seeds

Finishing Touches:

1/2 cup basil leaves chiffonade (shredded)

1/2 cup tomato concasse (chopped into small cubes)

a selection of garden vegetables (blanched and ready to use)

1/2 tsp. cracked black pepper (or to taste)

1/4 cup heavy cream

Method

For this recipe select the best available fresh fish and shellfish. Include any number of the following: Mussels, Scallops, Shrimp, Lobster, Sea Urchin, Dolphin, Red Snapper, Salmon, Kingfish.
(The fish should be cut to size depending on its density and cooking time. Vary the size of the cuts for presentation)
(1) Place all broth ingredients into a heavy based saucepan and cook until reduced by half.
(2) Into this reduction add the mussels and cover with a tight fitting lid. Bring to a quick boil over a high flame and shake saucepan vigorously to distribute heat evenly through the mussels.
(3) When the mussels open, remove them and set aside. Strain the remaining broth and return it to the saucepan.
(4) Gently poach the remaining fish and shellfish in the broth until warmed through. Add the selection of garden vegetables, cream, basil & tomato and cooked mussels. Season to taste and serve.

N.B. No salt should be needed, as mussels tend to be salty.

39 steps

The atmosphere at 39 Steps is pleasantly sophisticated and comfortably informal – with progressive music selections and live jazz every other Saturday night.

Opened in 1990 by Austrian chef, Josef Schwaiger, 39 Steps is located in a quaint wooden building which has been designed around the theme of traditional chattel house architecture. The newly renovated bistro offers lunch and dinner on a breezy, canopied balcony overlooking adjacent gardens with a view to the sea. In true bistro style, guests can enjoy an interesting menu that ranges from after-work 'tapas' style snacks to full-course lunches and dinners. The atmosphere at 39 Steps is pleasantly sophisticated and comfortably informal – with progressive music selections and live jazz every other Saturday night.

Equally popular with both locals and visitors alike, the spacious Italian marble bar is a lively after-work gathering spot. The friendly and popular managers, Monica Boland and Lindsey Archer, are always around to make sure that pastas, thick New York strips, blackened fish and hand-made gourmet pizzas are all expertly prepared to order. The bar features an extensive, reasonably priced wine list and full cocktail service.

Above - Mozzarella & Tomato with Olive & Balsamic Vinegar Dressing
Opposite - Coconut Shrimp with Spicy Pepper Jelly Sauce

Opposite - Vegetable Tempura with Soy & Mango Chutney
Above left - 39 Steps Special Traditional Steak & Kidney Pie
Above right - Goat Cheese, Black Olive, Tomato & Fresh Basil Pizza

Guava Pavlova with Maple Almond Ice Cream

The two Barbadian born chefs at 39 Steps, Sophia Crawford and Claudette Watson, were both trained by chef-owner Josef Schwaiger – who continually visits the kitchen to collaborate on menu updates and innovations. Austrian born Josef Schwaiger has lived and worked in Barbados for almost 20 years. One of Barbados' best-known chefs, he is also the man who first opened The Mews in Holetown, as well as his signature restaurant, Josef's in St. Lawrence Gap. An avid skier, Schwaiger is an intrepid traveller who says his favorite restaurants outside of Barbados are the Panhans in his hometown of Semmering, Austria and La Lunita in the small beach town of Akumal, Mexico. He also loves deep sea fishing and gardening and both of these past-times are sources of inspiration and material for new recipes.

Chef Josef Schwaiger's philosophy on food and wine: "Freshness. Always start from whatever is fresh on the market and work from there. I love the local ingredients from Barbados ... and it has improved so much here since we first began – you can really get all the world-class ingredients now. As far as wine goes, that of course is a passion – my favorites tend toward the old world wines – you just can't beat a nice Brouilly with our Escargots a la Bourguignonne and some crusty French bread; or a super-chilled Dom with our Seafood Antipasto."

Coconut Shrimp

Ingredients:

12 large shrimps
1 cup grated coconut
I cup corn flour
Pinch cayenne pepper
Salt & black pepper
2 egg whites, beaten

Method:

Peel 12 large shrimps but leave on the tails.

To roast the coconut: Place 1 cup grated coconut on a baking tray and roast in a 350 degree oven until brown.

To make the batter: Mix 1 cup corn flour with a pinch cayenne pepper, salt & black pepper and 2 beaten egg whites.

To prepare the shrimp: Dip each shrimp first into the cornflour mixture, then the egg whites and finally the roasted coconut.

Deep fry the shrimps until light brown. Serve with pepper jelly.

the tides

The Tides is located right on the sea, sitting as close to the water's edge as is possible for any restaurant in Barbados. An open dining terrace runs the full length of the restaurant and affords each table a clear view of the beautiful seascape.

Very aptly named, The Tides is located right on the sea, sitting as close to the water's edge as is possible for any restaurant in Barbados. To maximize this idyllic location, Guy and Tammie Beasley, the successful husband and wife team who opened The Tides in 2000, have created an open dining terrace that runs the full length of the restaurant and so affords each table a clear view of the beautiful seascape. Converted from a former house built out of traditional Barbadian coral stone, The Tides is neatly nestled in a flourishing landscaped garden, which adds another pleasing aspect to this attractive and homely restaurant.

Opposite - Crispy Duck, Seared Bay Scallops and Chorizo Sausage with a Lentil Vinaigrette on a Rocket & Red Leaf Salad

Above - Homemade Tartlet of Jumbo Shrimp, Atlantic Mussels, Bay Scallops & Calamari poached in a Snow Crab & Leek Cream

Previous page left - Smoked Salmon & Seared Bay Scallop in a Filo Mille Feuille with a Grainy Mustard Cream Sauce

Previuos page right - Coconut Chicken served with Sweet Potato Fries, Grilled Plantain & Banana Salsa

Above - Caramalized French Lemon Tart with Raspberry Coulis

Opposite - Homemade Panna Cotta with Champagne poached Fresh Strawberries and Sugar Lattice

Born in England, Chef Guy Beasley trained under the renowned Roux brothers in London and worked at their signature restaurant, the Michelin 3 Star 'Le Gavroche'. It was at this time that he met his future wife, Tammie, a Trini-Barbadian who also worked for the Roux brothers. The couple married in 1991 and came to live in Barbados, where Guy first worked as Executive Chef at the Royal Pavilion Hotel. In late 1994 the Beasleys teamed up to open their first restaurant, 'Putters on the Green', at the Sandy Lane Golf Club. As successful as 'Putters' was, Guy and Tammie still had aspirations of opening their own 'dream restaurant'; namely a restaurant next to the sea that served good food and provided good value for money, was elegant without being too pretentious, was friendly and welcoming in a relaxed Caribbean sort of way, and where people would feel very comfortable about just popping in for something to eat. Today their dream restaurant is a reality in the form of The Tides'.

The restaurant manager Trevor Parris, who is the epitome of Bajan charm and natural warmth, has a wealth of experience from his days at Sandy Lane and he works hard with the entire Tides team to ensure that all their guests are well looked after and made to feel very much at home. All the staff at Tides are proud of the personal touch that they add to every person's dining experience.

Guy draws upon the French influence from the early days of his training to create his own fusion of French, Italian, Caribbean, Asian and other cuisines. While Guy's strength is his light and tasty sauces, he also has a special touch with delicious desserts, such as 'Hot Chocolate Raspberry Souffle'.

In creating their wine list, Guy and Tammie are careful to offer a selection that ranges from 'the more affordable' right up to 'premier cru' classics.

Panna Cotta Champagne Strawberries

Ingredients

For the Panna Cotta:
1 vanilla pod – split length ways
10fl oz fresh milk
10fl oz heavy cream
1 1/2 teaspoons powdered gelatin
4oz white castor sugar

For the Poached Strawberries:
1lb fresh strawberries
4oz sugar
Zest of 1 orange & 1 lime
1/2 bottle dry champagne

For the Caramel Lattice:
3oz caster sugar
1oz water

Method

To Make the Panna Cotta

Bring to boil the milk, heavy cream, vanilla pod with seed scraped into the mixture and castor sugar. Meanwhile, mix gelatin with 3 tablespoons of cold water. Set aside to dissolve for 5 minutes then heat gelatin gently so the liquid is clear. Remove the milk and cream mixture from heat. Squeeze out the vanilla pod to extract all the flavour. Thoroughly mix in the warm gelatin into the milk, vanilla, cream and sugar. Pour into 6 lightly oiled ramekins and allow to set in a fridge.

To Make Poached Strawberries

Blanche the orange and lime zests twice. Add both zests to the champagne and 4oz sugar. Bring to boil. Remove from heat and add hulled, washed strawberries. Allow to cool in fridge.

To Make Caramel Lattice

For the caramel lattice, place 3oz castor sugar and 1oz water in very a clean, small pan. Bring to boil gently to dissolve sugar. Allow sugar to boil and turn to rich caramel colour. Remove pan from heat and dunk bottom of pan into a water bath. This stops the caramel from cooking and colouring further. Using a dinner fork, drizzle the caramel on to a well-oiled plate to create the lattice effect.

To Serve Panna Cotta

Gently tip the Panna Cotta cream into a shallow soup bowl. Decorate with chilled, poached strawberries and cooking liquor. Finally, finish with caramel lattice on top.

the waterfront café

Located on the banks of the Careenage in Bridgetown, this waterside restaurant has established a prominent niche in the Barbadian entertainment scene.

In September 1984, the Waterfront Café opened its doors on the banks of the Careenage in Bridgetown to an overwhelming turn out. They came by car, they came by foot and they even came by boat! Eighteen years hence, this waterside restaurant is still as exciting, as unpredictable and as inspiring as at her inception.

Created, owned and operated by Susan Walcott, along with her wonderful support team, The Waterfront, as she is affectionately known, has established a prominent niche in the Barbadian entertainment scene that is as strong today as it was in the very beginning. Musical entertainment is a daily feature at the Café, with some of the local "Jazz Greats" still wooing the hearts of patrons and setting the Café in a league of its own when it comes down to 'joie de vivre ' and atmosphere. The Waterfront has even had more than its fair share of celebrity guest appearances from international jazz artistes such as Bradford Marsalis, Dizzy Gillespie, Marcus Miller, Courtney Pine, Brenda Russell, Roberta Flack, Dave Koz and Kenny Ball. In addition to music, the Waterfront has also become something of a cultural hub for locals to showcase their works in poetry and art.

Above - Seafood Antipasti: a delightful combination platter of Smoked Flying Fish, King Fish Ceviche, Prawns, Melts, Crab Rissoles

Opposite - Steamed Flying Fish & Cou-Cou with Fried Plantain

Opposite - Calypso Seafood flamed with Pernod and finished with a Spicy Tomato Broth

Above left - Ceviche of King Fish • Above right - Windward Chicken Salad with Honey, Lime & Nut Vinaigrette

Opposite - Whole Snapper with Saffron Cream Sauce · Above - Spiced Chicken with Curry Chutney Sauce

The menu theme at the Waterfront was to create a restaurant where patrons could eat Caribbean specialties and tasty treats in very comfortable and relaxed surroundings. This philosophy of offering local cuisine was formulated by a very simple calculation. If you go to Italy you eat pasta; in the south of France you eat bouillabaisse; in Spain paella. So, when in Barbados, wouldn't you like to try flying fish melts, cornmeal cou cou or callaloo soup?

All of the cooks at the Waterfront are trained on the job by consultant and resident chefs, thus adding culinary expertise to their natural Bajan flair for preparing good, wholesome, tasty food.

Calypso Seafood
Serves 2

Ingredients:
8 oz Dolphin fillets, cut into 6 large cubes
6 only Large Shrimp, shelled and de-veined
6 only Sea Scallops
1/2 cup Pernod
1/2 cup Clamato Juice
2 tbsp Olive Oil
1/2cup Chopped onion, garlic and fresh herbs

Method:
In a saucepan, heat the olive oil and add the onion, garlic and fresh herbs. Sauté until opaque. Add the fish cubes, sealing all sides. Place the scallops and shrimp in the pan and sear until sealed.
Flame the pan with Pernod to de-glaze.
Remove the shrimp and set aside on hot serving plate.
Add clamato juice to the pan and finish cooking the fish and scallops.
Pour the contents into a serving dish with the shrimp and serve.

villa nova

Set in 15 acres of forested gardens on a wooded hilltop in St.John, with views across to the east coast, Villa Nova offers the ultimate in charm, relaxed sophistication and tranquility.

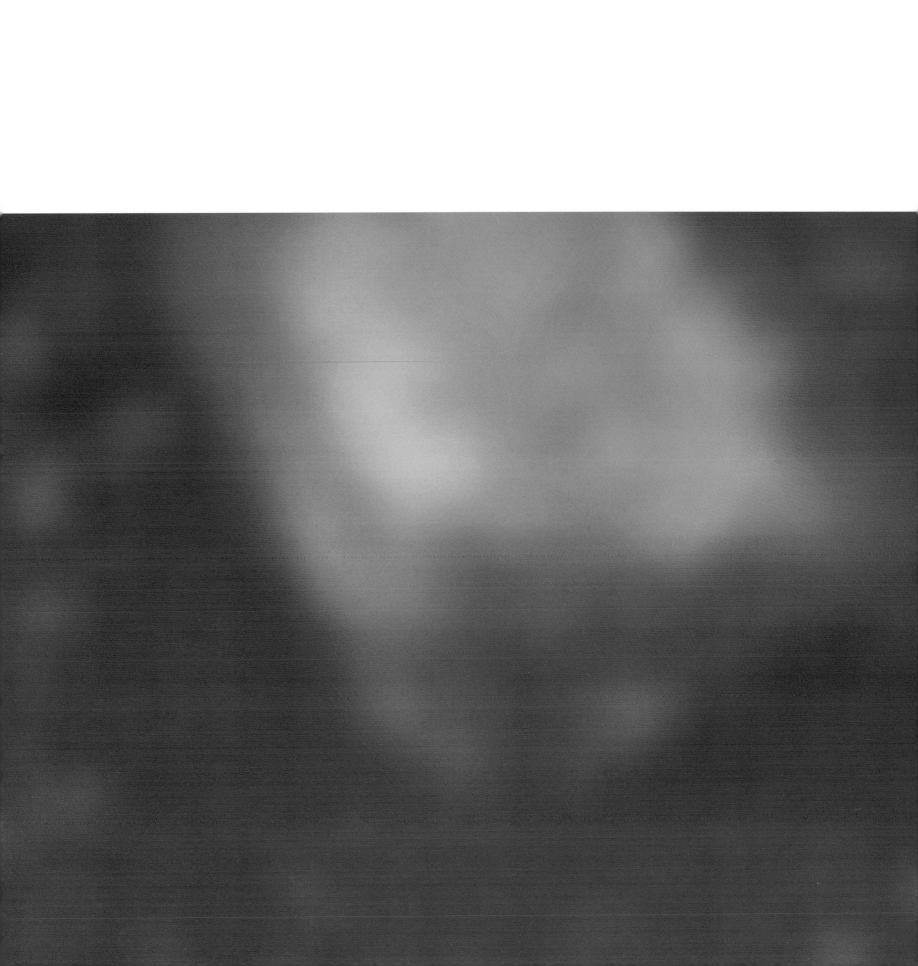

Set in 15 acres of forested gardens on a wooded hilltop in St.John, with views across to the east coast, Villa Nova offers the ultimate in charm, relaxed sophistication and tranquility. Since opening in April 2001, the dining room has established itself as a destination restaurant for both locals and visitors. Steeped in history, this classic coral stone plantation house, now a 27 suite hotel, was built in 1834 and was once home to British Prime Minister Sir Anthony Eden; whose many distinguished guests included Sir Winston Churchill and Her Majesty Queen Elizabeth II.

Wherever you sit in Villa Nova, be it on the terrace or in the restaurant, you are always within touching distance of the beauty of the incredibly lush garden and its impressive collection of mature trees. It is truly a pleasure to linger over a cocktail on the terrace or sip a glass of champagne in the lounge, before being shown to your table. For special occasions, Villa Nova can also provide a variety of optional dining areas, ranging from private dining rooms to a gazebo in the garden.

The intoxicating setting of Villa Nova is complemented by the flavours and presentation of the food prepared by award winning local chef, René Griffith. The menu of Caribbean fusion dishes takes advantage of the wonderful fresh produce available locally, combining the essence of the Caribbean with international favourites.

Opposite - Garden Salad with Blue Cheese, Pistachio Nuts and Balsamic Vinaigrette
Above left - Lamb loin wrapped in a Cashew Nut Mousse with Red Currant Reduction
Above right - Red Snapper with Wilted Spinach and Sauce Verge

Opposite - Grilled Beef Tournedos with Red Wine Jus

Above - Grilled Mahi Mahi with Shrimp in Crispy Noodle Wrap with Wilted Spinach and Sauce Verge

Following page left - Coriander Tuna with Ponzu

Following page right - Dark Chocolate and Orange Mousse with Wild Berry Compote.

Chef René Griffith, who began his career at the tender age of 14 has trained and worked in some of the best kitchens in Barbados, as well as spending time overseas fine-tuning his considerable culinary talents. An easy going man, he cites Marco Pierre White and Raymond Blanc as his heroes, not only for their skills as chefs but for their passion and belief in their art. It is a belief that Renée holds dear as he focuses on the creation of dishes that look just as good as they taste. He compares the presentation of food to the look of a pretty woman and believes that a dish should be presented in a way that enhances the flavours and textures of the food, so it as pleasing to the eye as it is to the palate. Good looking food you just have to eat!

Still only 29, Rene's ambition is to become one of the leading executive chefs in Barbados and the Caribbean. Preparing food is his passion and he continues to develop his craft to create truly inspirational cuisine.

Pan Roasted Lamb wrapped with Cashew Nut Mousse and Lentil Dahl
Serves 2

Ingredients
10oz lamb loin
3oz cashew nuts
8oz chicken breast
1 pinch marjoram
1 whole egg
2 tbsp oil
2oz heavy cream
4oz Puy lentils
1/2 oz onion
1oz tomato
1oz spinach leaves
1 pinch cilantro (chopped)
1/2 cup coconut milk
1 pinch curry powder
1 pinch Thai curry paste
1/2 oz garlic (chopped)
Salt & pepper to taste

Method
For the Lamb Loin:
Remove the sinew from the loin, season. Place oil in frying pan until hot, sear meat and leave to cool. Blanche the spinach in boiling water, then cool in ice water to retain the green colour. Place on cloth to dry.

For the Mousse:
Roughly dice the chicken breast and place in Robo Coupe with cashew nuts, egg and cream. Blend until smooth and season.

For the Lentils:
Place in boiling water and cook until firm. Remove and cool. Dice onions and tomatoes. Place oil in sauté pan just to coat. Add all herbs and vegetables, then curry powder and Thai curry paste, coconut milk, then lentils. Reduce until thickened, taking care not to over cook the lentils. Correct seasoning and serve.

To prepare the lamb:
Make a spinach mat and roll the lamb in spinach. Place plastic wrap sheet on table, then using a spatula, paste the mousse on the plastic evenly. Place lamb on the mousse and wrap tightly, then place in foil.

To serve:
Place the lamb in poaching water for 5-6 minutes. Arrange the lentils in a ring on a 12in. plate. Slice the lamb as desired and rest on top of the lentils.